THE ART OF COARSE GOLF

Also in Arrow by Michael Green

Michael Green

THE ART OF COARSE GOLF

Illustrated by John Jensen

ARROW BOOKS

Arrow Books Limited
17-21 Conway Street, London W1P 6JD

An imprint of the Hutchinson Publishing Group

London Melbourne Sydney Auckland
Johannesburg and agencies
throughout the world

First published by Hutchinson 1967
Arrow edition 1971
Reprinted 1975, 1976, 1978, 1982 and 1983
© Michael Green 1967 and 1970
Illustrations © Hutchinson Ltd 1967

Set in Monotype Baskerville

Printed and bound in Great Britain by
Anchor Brendon Ltd, Tiptree, Essex

ISBN 0 09 909940 3

For Steve and Nigel
with apologies for any understatement

Contents

Author's Note

I am indebted to Mr. N. Batley for permission to insult him in Chapter 7. Mr. Arnold Palmer, who is insulted in Chapter 9, did not give permission but I'm grateful just the same.

Two or three incidents described in this book also appeared in *The Art of Coarse Sport*. Don't let that stop anyone buying it.

Since this modest volume was first published some of the Rules of Golf have changed. I haven't altered the text however, as (a) I never did know the blasted rules anyway and (b) they keep on changing them.

Michael Green
The Bunkers
Chipping Badly
(expelled London Scottish Golf Club 1970)

I

An Introduction to Coarse Golf

'Now they lie
In centuries of sand beside the church.
Less pitiable are they than the corpse
Of a large golfer, only four weeks dead. . . .'

JOHN BETJEMAN

The only time in my life I looked like winning a golf competition I was swindled out of it by twenty Irish navvies.

It was the office stroke-play tournament, for which we used a course near London. Inconceivable though it may seem to those who know me, everyone else was playing worse than me, and by the thirteenth I was bulging with self-satisfaction. So much so, that I recklessly decided to use my driver for the first time in two years.

In this frame of mind I didn't bother with all that pedantic stuff about keeping the head down and the left elbow straight, and when I drove the ball screeched into a nearby road and disappeared through the window of a passing lorry.

The lorry swerved across the road and stopped violently. Twenty of the largest men I have ever seen in my life promptly shot over the side.

I was naturally very distressed to see them sprawling all over the road and was just about to go over and apologise (and if possible get back the ball) when a vast, shambling creature arose, crossing himself, and said in a loud Irish voice, 'I'm going to murder him.'

At this a low mumbling arose, in the middle of which I could distinguish someone saying, 'That's right, Pat, let's fill him in.'

'He means you,' said my opponent, walking hastily down the fairway, the rat. I hurriedly put down another ball, struck it swiftly in the vague direction of the green, and hastened after him.

Luckily a spinney hid us from view by now and at the end of the next hole, which took us back into the country, I was recovering. But just as I was addressing the ball at the short fifteenth a lorry drew up on the road behind the tee and a fist was shaken violently over the hedge.

It was then I discovered the secret of perfect golf. Fear.

A quick flash of my seven iron and the ball was skimming to the green. I moved so quickly I nearly got there before it landed. Even then it was a near thing. As the last putt dropped there came the sound of an engine revving and I saw the lorry trying to get through a gate on to the course.

'If I were you,' said my opponent, 'I'd turn my collar round and pretend to be a priest.'

At the sixteenth several Irishmen actually burst through the hedge but fortunately I was searching for my ball in a stream and hid under a friendly bridge until they retreated, jabbering to each other. At the seventeenth the lorry sped by the green and a brick was thrown at me. Then they all vanished.

I breathed a sigh of relief and concentrated on winning. As long as I got round in a hundred or so it was a certainty.

The last hole was a short one, sloping upwards towards the clubhouse. My drive was a corking 95 yards and with only another 60 yards to go I had four strokes in hand to break 100. The tournament was as good as mine!

I was just strolling up the fairway wondering whether I could make the green in two strokes when the lorry appeared on the skyline and screamed to a halt in front of the professional's shop. Here it vomited a score of Irishmen who started swarming all over the eighteenth green, covering it with cigarette ends and wiping their boots on the turf.

It was too much. We turned and fled.

After about an hour we became tired of skulking in a bus shelter and jumping three feet every time a lorry went by, so we telephoned the clubhouse. The steward told us that the Irishmen refused to go away and he was out of draught Guinness. He advised me to keep clear.

It was dark before we sneaked back. Then they told me that if I had returned on time I would have won the competition easily but after waiting until eight o'clock they had given the cup to someone else who went round in 105.

I suppose that experience isn't really anything to do with the actual game of golf. But then, Coarse Golfers' most vivid memories never are.

Ask the average six-handicap man his greatest experience and he will reply without hesitation that it was the time he holed in one on the notorious thirteenth at Muirfield, and what is more if you care to stand back he can remember exactly what he did with his swing.

But most of us have no holes-in-one or albatrosses to dream over, merely memories involving terrible humiliations, of pursuit by angry gardeners clutching their bruised heads when we ask for our ball back, or the crash of breaking glass that follows the use of a three wood off the fairway.

We are the Coarse Golfers of the world.

It took me thirty years to realise that I was a Coarse Golfer. Like the great Vardon, who learned his golf as a youngster with home-made clubs and marbles for balls, I became a devotee at an early age.

The game first cast its spell on me as a child in the 1930's. Four of us, evil, mischievous children, used to play on the local golf course. But not golf. Courses were less crowded in those days, even on Sundays, and there was little chance of anyone stopping us as we buried each other in bunkers, chased each other across the greens and quietly rolled balls into unplayable lies on the pretext of helping search for them.

I suppose this shows that even then I had a certain instinct for the game. At any rate I could see that when a ball was underneath a bush or just in front of a tuft the striker turned red and said the word Mother had forbidden any of us to use. Sometimes they said other words which I did not recognise and which I repeated at home with disastrous results.

As time passed I became expert at finding a ball in the rough and casually flicking it with my foot behind a tree before I cried out, 'Here you are, mister, I've found it.' Sometimes the poor fools even rewarded us with a penny.

But our cruellest trick was at a hole bordered by a thick spinney. There we would crouch behind the bushes as red-faced old men in plus-fours stood on the tee. In those days all golfers were elderly, with red faces and purple noses. They smoked pipes, wore plus-fours and drove Rileys with tin GB plates.

As the player started his final downswing four healthy young lungs would erupt into a chorus of loud and phlegmatic coughing, ending with a ghastly retch that suggested a platoon of infantry vomiting behind the bush.

Reactions varied. If the ball went straight the interruption might be ignored. At other times it would go screaming over the woods and the golfers would march menacingly into the bushes as we fled for safety.

But even as a child I noticed that it was the man who made the stroke who was most annoyed. If there were four golfers playing, two of them often had great difficulty in not looking pleased and once a man even pressed sixpence into my hand.

Time passed. I gave up playing on the golf course in favour of cricket and girls, and then a few years later started playing on it again, this time with clubs, although the results weren't very different from my childhood activities. After four years I still hadn't broken 100 so I changed my grip, which had previously been based on a diagram in a book on how to play cricket.

This brought about a dramatic improvement. I knocked 36 strokes off my game—from 145 to 109. Obviously something was still wrong.

It was then that a terrible thought came into my mind. I became convinced that I was being punished for what I had done as a child.

It seemed clear that the plus-foured souls of those red-faced golfers had in due course ascended to the Greater Clubhouse on High, whence they looked down and were getting their revenge by directing malevolent beams towards me as I drove and putted.

This deep-rooted sense of guilt weighed with me for years until finally reason took over. After all, there were plenty of other people whose drives hit their opponents and who, when they said they'd done a hole in two, meant they'd only lost two balls.

And then I realised that the real reason for my failure was simply that I was by nature a Coarse Golfer.

Perhaps I should explain exactly what is meant by coarse. Those who have read my other works on such coarse activities as rugby, sailing and amateur dramatics, will need no explanation. Firstly, it must be explained that the adjective 'coarse' in this connection has nothing to do with spilling egg on your tie or eating soup with a knife.

It is not so much an attitude to life, as the attitude of life to a person. It is we coarse people who lost all our marbles at school, whose bicycle chains kept coming off, whose roofs leak, whose pipes freeze.

A simple test of coarseness in life might be as follows :

Do garage mechanics call you 'sir'? Or 'squire', 'friend', 'mate' and 'filth'?

Do they repair the car properly?

Do they advise you to take it somewhere else?

Do they kick it contemptuously?

Do bus conductors call you 'chum'?

Do bank managers roar with laughter when you want a loan?

Applied to golf a similar test would be :

Have you ever five-putted?

Have you ever been warned off a golf course?

Do friends ring you up to play?

Have you ever made an air-shot on the green?

Have you ever taken double figures to get out of a bunker?

Have you ever broken 100?

Have you ever broken anything else?

When playing alone are you regularly overtaken by women's foursomes?

I have given a lot of thought to defining accurately a Coarse Golfer, and have decided that the following is probably the best definition :

'A Coarse Golfer is one who normally goes from tee to green without touching the fairway.'

I feel that definition sums up the spirit of Coarse Golf, the terrible loneliness of the long-distance Coarse Golfer, his separateness not only from other golfers but from the rest of the golf course as well.

There are, however, other definitions which help, among which I like best : 'One who has to shout "Fore" when he putts.'

Others that spring to mind are 'One who only counts the strokes when he actually hits the ball' and 'A man who always needs one more club.'

But however one may define a Coarse Golfer, there is one infallible way of identifying him, and that is by his divots, which are spaced extremely close together, sometimes no more than a few paces from each other.

One who has to shout 'Fore' when he putts

It is usually impossible for a Coarse Golfer to fill up his divot adequately, as he tends to cause a minor explosion which sends pieces of earth in all directions, so the presence of a Coarse Golfer can be discovered by small craters scattered at frequent intervals on the course, rather as if a shower of tiny meteorites had landed.

Indeed, connoisseurs are often able to identify individual players by the shape of their divots and their frequency. My friend Askew claims he always knows when I have been playing by my habit of leaving peculiar little pear-shaped marks at thirty-yard intervals.

Coarse players exist in all branches of sport but there is a big difference between the Coarse Golfer and his counterpart elsewhere. For golf is the one sport which erects a barrier between those who can and those who can't. It is not a game with the infinitely subtle variations of inefficiency which exist in other sports.

Take rugby for instance. At one end of the scale are giants with thighs like oak trees, who break three ribs, have them roughly strapped up, and return to run eighty yards and score the winning try. At the other end are pimply adolescents feebly chasing each other in a barren meadow at the end of the Piccadilly Line.

But the Rugby Union recognises the existence of both types. The same laws apply to both of them, and if the giant is having a run-out after breaking both legs, he might find himself in the same team as the weed of the Extra C₍

It's the same in cricket, hockey, tennis, soccer, almost every other sport. But not in golf. Unless you can play to a handicap of twenty-four you don't even exist according to the Royal and Ancient. And if you *can* play to twenty-four you still don't exist unless you join a club to prove it.

The result is that golf has a vast army of invisible players, the shadow battalions that may be seen hacking their way round almost any course, their progress marked by flying clods and despairing oaths.

What is forgotten, however, is that counting those who are a nominal twenty-four, but who only achieved it by dropping three fake cards in the handicap box, the invisible golfers probably outnumber the others by two to one. It's just hypocrisy to pretend that two-thirds of the world's golfers don't even exist.

Then there's this term 'handicap player' used disparagingly by golf writers to mean someone who's no good. They don't understand that to a Coarse Golfer 'handicap players' is a term of high praise—it means someone who is actually good enough to have a handicap.

In this respect one must applaud the Ladies' Golf Union, whose handicaps go up to a sensible thirty-six. Despairing of ever receiving a handicap, I once applied to join the L.G.U., hoping they would at least give me thirty-six, but my application was rejected, not because I am a man, but because I couldn't play to thirty-six.

The following chart will put matters in their true perspective:

HANDICAP	OFFICIAL DEFINITION	TRUTH
40	A human rat who should be thrown off every course	The backbone of the game. A splendid fellow who will give you an enjoyable round and who undoubtedly has that generous interpretation of the rules which is the mark of the gentleman
35	Does not exist	The ideal opponent. Always a tough game. Probably a golf writer
24	Rabbit	Rather a tiger. Avoid him. Although ten strokes better than you he won't concede any. May be pedantic about little things like not counting air shots
19	Rabbit	A leopard. This man may actually have won a competition
12	A mere handicap player	A positive jaguar. But don't worry, he wouldn't want to play with you
Scratch	A useful golfer	These people do not exist outside television screens

The fact is, of course, that those with low handicaps are not merely better golfers than the others. They live in a different world and play a totally different game.

It would do some of them good to visit parts of the course they have never seen, quarries and jungles and thickets they don't know exist. Most of them haven't the remotest idea what a decent piece of rough looks like. It would teach them a lot to have to retrieve some of the situations which a Coarse Golfer gets into.

The whole handicap business is typical of the hypocrisy which surrounds golf and which the Coase Golfer must shake off if he is to survive.

One of the common fallacies is that golf breeds wonderful friendships and sportsmanship. One has only to watch the face of a man missing a two-foot putt in the Open on television to see how far *that* is from the truth. Indeed, as far as making friends goes, golf is the finest game in the world for making enemies.

Oddly enough, while it isn't difficult to make friends in this world, it's extraordinarily difficult to make a good enemy. But by George you can do it through golf. The game's capacity for arousing hatred is greatly underestimated.

Indeed, I have a friend whose father has not spoken to him for three years since the son, partnering him in a competition, was left with an eighteen-inch putt to win the Autumn Cup. While nervously adjusting his feet for the vital stroke he accidentally trod on their opponents' ball and the subsequent penalty cost them the hole, the match, the cup, and their entire family life.

Why golf is being taught in schools I cannot imagine. It is essentially a selfish game and can only encourage self-aggrandisement in the successful and deep inferiority in the unsuccessful. Golf is obsessional, vile, encourages gambling on the course and in the clubhouse, leads to bad language, the expenditure of a great deal of money (most of it wasted) and has wrecked many marriages.

I cannot understand why anyone plays it. In fact the only reason I am spending my holidays golfing this year is because I'm convinced that with a bit of practice I can cure my hook. I'm sure I'm standing too close to the ball and relaxing the knees too much. I think that if I took up a more open stance and moved the front foot . . .

Which, of course, is the whole trouble. You can't stop playing the game. Surely there must be a way to stop playing golf? That's what is needed instead of all these instructional books on how to play, a walloping good book on how to give it up.

To crown it all, the worse one is at golf, the more obsessional it becomes. It's a complete fallacy that it's the boys who are fifteen handicap who worry about getting down into single figures. They don't care a damn. It's the Coarse Golfer who becomes fixated, usually about breaking a hundred. He doesn't worry about having his handicap reduced—he just wants to get one. Even winning is secondary to getting round the course without disgracing himself and receiving pitying smiles.

It is strange the exaggerated importance that people place on prowess at golf. Go into a clubhouse and say you regularly commit adultery and they'll all roar with laughter, except those who want the address of the woman. But say you just went round in 102 and people start edging away and looking down their noses.

Some years ago I used to play with a Jewish friend called Sammy, who was always the butt of the club humorist, whose idea of wit was to finger Sammy's lapel and say, 'Nice bit of cloth you've got there, my boy', in a Fagin-type accent. Sammy took it all with considerable patience until one day there was a terrible row in the locker room and we rushed in there to find Sammy trying to strangle the man.

After parting them we enquired the reason.

'He kept criticising my grip,' snarled Sammy. 'I couldn't stand it any more.'

This, then, is the jungle which the Coarse Golfer must enter. He is ill-equipped for the task, because besides having little skill he is probably a truthful person. And in golf, as in war, the first casualty is truth.

One of the strange thing about games, and golf in particular, is that people who are really bad or good are invariably honest, while those in between are thundering liars. Just watch any golf game and compare it with the bar conversation afterwards. The greatest untruths in golf are compounded by those with handicaps between 6 and 18.

To make matters worse, a Coarse Golfer can be his own enemy. For years I played with a man who was firmly under the impression that air shots counted as *two* strokes. As a result, he was often four strokes down before he left the tee.

With the cards stacked against him so heavily, the Coarse Golfer is therefore entitled to employ certain tricks and wheezes, merely to survive. But remember, the difference between a cheat and a Coarse Golfer is that the Coarse Golfer usually cheats within the rules.

2

Drawn from Life

'Many a heart is aching,
   If you could read them all,
   Many the hopes that have vanished,
   After the ball.'

CHARLES K. HARRIS

It is a wet Wednesday afternoon not far from the North
Circular Road. The United British Corsets Ltd. Golfing Society are holding their autumn meeting. There is
some confusion as to the form this is to take. The first
four players off understood it was to be a Stableford,
but it has since been discovered that no one else knows
how to score in a Stableford, and the society captain
has told the others just to mark their cards up and
they'll decide how to pick the winner in the bar afterwards. He is in a hurry for them to get on with matters
as there are already loud complaints from club members at being held up by 'another of those damn society
meetings'.

At the present moment, four players are waiting
their turn to drive from the first. Three of them are

27

respectively Fatty, Lanky and Blood Pressure. These, of course, are not their real names but they are fair descriptions and the details can be filled in as we go along. The fourth player is completely out of place and we shall call him George.

George has just joined head office as an executive trainee straight from university. He used to go round the Gog and Magog at Cambridge in the high eighties and back home in Hampshire his handicap is 19. It is his first game for the firm and after hearing the confident way everyone talked in the locker room he is very worried as to whether he will make the grade.

A pair are driving off in front of them. Lanky and Fatty are wildly swishing the air with their drivers, while Lanky voids himself of satisfied grunting noises and announces to all and sundry that he has at last cracked the game.

The player who is driving stops his address and looks round pointedly. Fatty and Lanky freeze into impossible positions of immobility. The player is aware out of the corner of his eye that two men are standing like something out of a cellar in the Louvre and wishes they would relax and let him concentrate.

As they show no signs of doing so he hopes for the best, takes a short backswing and sends the ball into a lateral water hazard on the left of the fairway. As he does so Fatty and Lanky relax with audible exhalations of breath, as if a couple of old cycle tyres were going down.

'Scrubbers,' says Blood Pressure fiercely, and they

all nod in agreement, because Blood Pressure is greatly admired by them all, having once had a handicap of 23 with a golf club in Sussex. 'We'll go through them in a minute, never fear. I think it's your right to show us the way.'

They have not in fact tossed a coin, but in any case Blood Pressure is sales manager and his word is law. Fatty does not fancy letting himself down in front of the clubhouse, but he reluctantly drags himself forward, tees up his ball and peers hopefully into the distance.

'Better let 'em get on a bit,' he mutters, 'I might hit 'em if I connect properly.' (The pair in front are three hundred yards away.) He waits until they are on the green, when a sudden and terrible change comes over him. His eyes widen in a ghastly stare, veins stand out all over his face and his whole body becomes completely rigid.

Still rigid he hunches himself forward, his legs wide apart, towards the ball. Four feet from it he stops, and slowly bends his legs until he is in a semi-squatting posture, with the seat of his trousers about two feet from the ground. He then stamps the ground twice like Rumpelstiltskin. After remaining in this uncomfortable and slightly obscene posture for some moments he lifts the club back round his neck in a low, flat swing like a ruptured man lifting a heavy weight, and lets fly.

The ball travels 100 yards off the toe of the club and lands in a small copse on the right of the fairway, while Fatty staggers about the tee like a drunken man.

George, who feels he ought to get a reputation as a good fellow, murmurs 'Bad luck' sympathetically.

To his astonishment Fatty turns to the others in triumph.

'Beat that,' he snarls and takes up a position of easy confidence, casually leaning on his club at the edge of the tee and muttering to himself.

The others are by no means confident that they can.

Lanky now takes up his stance. This is slightly unusual, inasmuch as he is facing at right angles to the hole, and people at the side of the tee move away in alarm. Lanky, however, is merely compensating for his slice. After a good deal of twitching and shuffling he picks up his tee, moves it three inches to the left and starts again. Suddenly, without warning, he winds himself up like a cheap alarm clock, utters a half-human shout, and in a whirl of thin limbs puts his ball into a nearby back garden, via the handle of someone's trolley.

Blood Pressure's turn. He looks professionally towards the hole several times and then at the ball, as if he is afraid someone is going to steal it.

When he is apparently satisfied that nobody is, he cautiously approaches it and remains silent and still for some minutes. Then he lifts his driver back very slowly until it is level with his waist and pauses. Finally, keeping every fibre of his body rigid, he lowers the club on to the ball which reluctantly leaves the tee and travels thirty yards in a dead straight line.

'I'm getting them away today,' he says complacently.

Meanwhile George has been watching with astonishment. He is young and inexperienced and hasn't seen anything like this before. His address is spoiled by the constant noise going on behind him on the tee, where Fatty and Blood Pressure are arguing in a loud whisper about the love-life of Fatty's secretary. Just as he has accustomed himself to the row there are loud cries of 'Ssh . . . ssh . . . quiet everyone . . . give the lad a chance' and the whispering is succeeded by a painful silence, broken only by heavy breathing.

George tries to collect his shattered concentration and swings a little desperately. The ball curves precariously over the rough but at the last minute fades back on to the fairway after travelling about 170 yards.

He is just stepping back rather crestfallen when he is surprised by an outbreak of noise among the others, who are exclaiming : 'Brilliant ! What a shot ! You've played before' . . . and so on. Blood Pressure adds, 'And the lad says his handicap's nineteen. I don't believe it.'

The four go their separate ways. George's offers to help search for balls are turned down and he hits a nice five iron to the apron without waiting for Blood Pressure who is jerking around somewhere near the ladies' tee.

Having reached the green in three George leans on his putter and waits. After ten minutes two women arrive on the green and pointedly ask if they can carry on, as he apparently doesn't intend to putt out. George agrees and asks if they have seen any signs of three physically deformed men playing the hole.

The women say no, although as they were driving from the ladies' plateau tee a red-faced man stuck his head over the front and was nearly decapitated. But they thought he was a greenkeeper.

While the women are putting there is a terrible humming noise like a six-inch shell in full flight and a ball thuds near the stick and vanishes at high speed into the rough behind the green. From behind a distant bush is heard a faint, despairing cry of 'Watch it someone, for heaven's sake.'

George apologises on behalf of his colleagues, pointing out that the ball was obviously played from a point where the striker could not see the green. The women are not amused and ask acidly why George's partners are skulking about behind bushes as if afraid to show themselves.

At that moment Lanky rushes out of some trees to one side of the green like a sex maniac in hot weather and vanishes into the bushes the other side without a word of explanation. The women depart, looking apprehensively about them.

Blood Pressure arrives on the green and is followed by Fatty who has branches and twigs all over him. At last they can putt out.

George takes two for a five. Lanky, who is assailed by a terrible fit of jerking, putts into a bunker, takes three to get out, and then adds four more putts. Fatty takes one putt, which rolls six feet past the hole, picks up his ball and says, 'Never bother to take those tiddlers when I'm playing with friends.'

Blood Pressure, who is nine feet from the hole, promptly picks up his ball and says, 'Me neither.'

Without leaving the green, the three take out their cards and pencils, ignoring distant cries of impatient protest from the first round of the Knock-Out Cup behind them.

'Afraid I took a five there,' announces Fatty.

There is a moment's silence during which George wonders if he is going insane.

'How do you make that out?' says Blood Pressure severely.

'Quite simple,' says Fatty. 'One into the wood, two out, three on the green and two putts—five.'

The sheer effrontery of this takes everyone's breath away, but Lanky recovers sufficiently to say, 'But I saw you swishing away like mad as I was climbing the garden fence to get my ball.'

'I was trying to kill a wounded bird,' replies Fatty promptly. 'I couldn't leave the poor thing in agony, could I? Killed it cleanly with a three iron on the back of the neck. Just a touch of slice, though. Must have been bending the elbow again.'

He turns to George, who is looking anxiously at the players gibbering behind.

'How many did you take?'

'Five.'

'Then we halve,' says Fatty with an air of finality. 'If I may presume, I think you took the wrong line on that first putt. The borrow is very tricky on this green. All right, all right, we're going.' The last sentence is prompted by the thud of a ball on the green as the Knock-Out Cup as last lose all patience.

Three and a half hours later it is still raining and from the clubhouse, which stands on a hill, it is just possible to discern four wet and weary figures playing the last hole in deep gloom. The Knock-Out Cup have long ago passed through and are now sitting round the clubhouse fire.

Spurts of sand, like little fountains, from the cross-bunker announce that Lanky is in some difficulty. Beside the ditch what appears to be a small fat mole is creeping along on all fours, peering into the water with shrill cries of dismay. On the fairway a tiny earthquake is going on, where Blood Pressure is solemnly proceeding fifty yards at a time. There is no sign of George who is the other side of the hedge, looking for Fatty's ball.

Blood Pressure is first on the green, long experience having taught him the futility of trying to help the others. He is followed by Lanky (via the roof of the professional's shop) and surprisingly by Fatty. George is not only last, but his six iron, normally so reliable, lands him a good forty yards to the left of the green. He walks up the hill and on reaching his ball waves to the others to play.

'No, you play,' shouts Blood Pressure, 'we're on the green.'

George replies that he, too, is on the green. He modestly adds that being a conventional type of person he prefers to finish the course on the eighteenth and not the thirteenth.

After ten minutes' argument, during which Fatty has to be restrained from chipping off the green, it is agreed that George can play out on his green and the others on theirs. Having done so they hasten through the rain to the clubhouse.

In the bar there is a certain amount of confusion. The harassed secretary of the United British Corsets Ltd. has rashly undertaken to work out everyone's Stableford score from their cards, since most of the players cannot be trusted to do it themselves. Blood Pressure says he will work out his own and announces it as 48. Fatty demands a recount and the secretary make it five, at which point Blood Pressure angrily denounces the whole competition as a fiddle.

The winner is eventually announced, with a score of 29 points. George, who knows perfectly well that he himself scored 33, does not bother to argue, but offers to buy Fatty a drink.

'Well,' says Fatty, his tongue loosened by the beer, 'I can't say I tamed the course, but I certainly showed it a touch of the whip, if I may put it that way. Ninety-four's not bad considering the conditions.'

According to George's private calculations, started at the second hole, Fatty has taken at least 115 strokes that he could see, not counting invisible and mysterious swishes in the undergrowth, and his Stableford total is one. But the last four hours have shown him a new world and he keeps quiet.

Blood Pressure and Lanky join the group.

'I thought our young friend here wasn't at all bad,' says Blood Pressure, nodding condescendingly at George. 'Perhaps a little uncertain off the tee, though.'

'I was going to mention that,' chimes in Fatty. 'You've got the classic hooker's grip, you know. It is a fault of all you young players. You can't see a knuckle when you drive. Took me years to cure myself. What you want to do, George, is to take a five iron before breakfast every morning and hold it in one hand and swing it forty times round your head. You'll find that gradually . . .'

And there it is time to leave them. The fantasies have taken over, truth has fled out of the door, and the course is diminishing in size with each drink. As for George, he won't play for them again, but will join a good club in Surrey where he will in time reach a single-figure handicap and play with real golfers.

But occasionally, in ten or twenty years' time, he will say in the bar, 'I don't know if I ever told you of a re-markable experience I had playing for the United British Corsets Ltd. Golf Society years ago . . . extra-ordinary crowd they were . . .'

So George will tell his tale. And nobody will believe a word.

3

Preparation and Equipment

'Club—kind of stick used in golf'
OXFORD ENGLISH DICTIONARY

While there are certain infallible signs that a Coarse
Golfer is at work, such as the closeness and rich quality
of the divots, or hoarse cries from underneath bridges,
it is not always possible to recognise a Coarse Golfer
by his equipment. A man with one of those vast coffin-
like bags with clubs and rods and nets and umbrellas
sticking out all over it might be a Coarse Golfer trying
to *look* as if he could play the game.

And that shabby creature hacking his way round
with a five iron and an old trilby hat is probably 'Tiger'
Tim Jones, the Terror of the Monthly Medal.

It is true, though, that many Coarse Golfers (especially the younger ones) will be found playing with
ancient clubs, dredged from some old attic where they
lay in peace among the old gramophone records and
square-handled tennis rackets. Often a Coarse Golfer
may be recognised by one relic of his earlier days, perhaps a putter shaped like a letter Z.

Golfers become very attached to the clubs with which they first learn to play. As my friend Askew told the police when his car was stolen with his clubs in the boot, 'I wish to report the loss of a valuable old five iron . . . well, there was a Jaguar car as well, but you've got to get that iron back. It's the only club I can use at the water-hole.'

My own first set of clubs were formerly in the possession of my Uncle Walter, who presented them to me many years ago when he gave up golf for the fourteenth time in his life.

They were wooden-shafted and came in a thin leather bag which collapsed when stood upright. Strange oaths like 'Mashie Niblick' were engraved on the face of each club. For a long time I imagined they must have belonged to an eccentric Scots miser, old Mashie Niblick ('Aye, Meestair Niblick, 'twas a fine idea to engrave your name on yon wee clubs. . . .')

I never really prospered with them, probably because they all had bits of twine and leather hanging from the shafts. When I played a stroke it looked like someone hoisting a distress signal. Yet I grew to love them and it was a great blow when I lost them in strange circumstances. I then lived in a town where it was necessary to put the dustbin out on the pavement for emptying and I left the clubs leaning against the bin while I waited for a lift.

Before the car came I had to go back indoors and when I returned the clubs had gone, along with the rest of the rubbish. A neighbour said she saw them sticking out of the back of the local dustcart and that was the last I heard of them.

'You was lucky they took them,' she said, 'because normally they won't take anything that's too big to go in the bin.'

Only one of the clubs survived. It was in such bad shape I'd left it in the house. The grip had rotted and been repaired at some time with carpenter's glue, so after two holes the warmth of the fingers caused the club to stick firmly to the hands.

After that I used to carry it round simply for the purpose of lending to opponents in trouble.

Golfers are highly susceptible to advice, no matter how bad, when they're in trouble. When my opponent was staring at the roots of a tree and wondering how on earth he could scrape out the ball I would approach, holding my old club gingerly by the head, and say, 'Try this old thing. It never fails.'

The opponent would always give it a trial swish at least, after which he spent the next five minutes desperately wiping his hands on the grass to get the glue off. He rarely succeeded, and somehow his game was never the same afterwards.

I mentioned this because it brings us to Law One of Coarse Golf, viz: 'The most important part of a Coarse Golfer's equipment is that which he keeps for lending to an opponent.'

It is one of the signs of the Coarse Golfer that he never has enough of everything he needs. This is not due to poverty but to his peculiar attitude to the game, a feeling that he may be giving it up at any minute so it's no use buying his balls by the dozen or investing in expensive waterproofs.

Indeed, I feel that one definition of a Coarse Golfer is a player who always buys his tees one at a time, and I don't think it would be far off the mark.

This situation can be turned to advantage by carrying in the bag a few items especially for lending to an opponent, with the intention of sabotaging his game.

My own equipment is modest enough but always includes the following things to lend:

> Several special balls
> A tee
> Ancient club
> Waterproof jacket and trousers
> A tin of sweets
> Packet of Greek cigarettes
> Empty ballpoint pen

Those who play other games will recognise this as a variation of the customs in Coarse Rugby and Hockey, when one side are two or three men short and the other team lend them a player. The player is, of course, invariably an incompetent half-wit who will thoroughly wreck their chances.

To go through the list in order: the lending balls should preferably have been recovered from the bottom of a ditch after lying there for six weeks. It is a good idea to have a separate compartment on the bag into which can be placed any old balls found in the rough or on the driving range, so one will not accidentally lend a good ball.

If you are fortunate enough to have a good collection of worn-out balls, ask an opponent to name the brand he would like. It is not necessary to mention that the ball has lain in the undergrowth for three months, and he will be made to look churlish if he rejects the gift.

The effect of hitting a ball apparently made of stone cannot be over-estimated.

It might be thought there would be little use for a lending tee, but this is not so. I find it is the item most frequently borrowed, especially if one is clever enough to pick up any tees lying around the course before your opponent finds them.

My lending tee is pale mauve and made of plastic. During its long life it has become permanently bent and blunted and will not stick in the earth in dry weather unless it is first straightened. If this is done it slowly starts to bend again with the result that the ball keeps falling off it.

The effect is increased if every time the ball falls off one says with a smile, 'Playing two, playing three', and so on.

A suitable waterproof jacket for lending should have sleeves so short that they prevent any free movement of the arms whatsoever. It is true that the striker will discard the jacket after one stroke but that stroke is likely to be worth a hole.

A further refinement is to suggest there is nothing wrong with the jacket, but that the player himself is deformed and has unnaturally long arms.

If waterproof trousers are used instead of a jacket, they must not have any means of being supported. With luck they will begin to slide down over the striker's hips as he addresses the ball.

He may either continue with the stroke, and court disaster, or stop and hitch them up. In this case, after hitching them up five or six times, his morale will be completely shattered. Alternatively, he may try to hold them up with one elbow while playing his stroke, with inevitable results.

Remember—they must not have any means of being supported

My friend Askew uses a more subtle variation, namely a waterproof jacket of great expense and supreme comfort, *which is not waterproof at all.* The effect is one of long, slow, drawn-out discomfort and damp.

Askew in his tortured way reckons that the jacket always wins him *the next game,* and there may well be something in that. Certainly one of his regular opponents has just given up golf for six months because of rheumatism.

Of all the items in a Coarse Golfer's equipment, the tin of sweets is easily the most important. I must explain immediately that they are not poisoned or doctored. All that is necessary is that they should be hard and dry, and the tin half-empty so they will rattle.

The method of use is as follows : Before driving from the first tee bring the sweets forth noisily and offer them around. This will make it plain that they *can* rattle. Then, when it is desired to affect an opponent's shot, bring them out and offer them again before his address. Do not replace them in the bag but hold the tin rigidly, with an expression showing that whatever happens you are *not* going to put off your opponent by letting them rattle.

He knows that they can rattle, he expects them to rattle, he is waiting for them to rattle, he almost wants them to rattle. What he doesn't anticipate is this agonising silence in which they are liable to rattle at any moment.

Let there be no doubt as to the effectiveness of this.

A man who was playing my Uncle Walter actually stopped in the middle of his downswing and bellowed, 'For God's sake, man, rattle them and get it over.' By this time his morale was so shattered that his drive entered a 65 bus and was carried on to Chessington Zoo.

'Bad luck,' murmured Uncle Walter, 'if it'd been a 37 they might have dropped it off by the green.'

I always call this device The Sweets of Damocles.

The carrying of a packet of Greek cigarettes for handing round should be self-explanatory. After lighting your own, do not inhale and take the first opportunity to throw it away (not near any living creature).

The empty ballpoint is for giving to an opponent to mark his card. Few things in golf equal the frustration of trying to write on a card by scratching its surface with a useless pen, especially if you've just lost the hole. Not only that, but the whole thing becomes a challenge to make the wretched pen work, if necessary by digging into the surface of the card. The nervous tension aroused by this compulsion is quite enough to wreck a complete hole, even a round if you're lucky.

A suitable alternative is a tiny stub of pencil, half an inch long, which is impossible to grasp properly. On handing it over, say merrily, 'Golfers who know, buy from their pro.' For some reason this always irritates people.

The above list is merely basic equipment. The experienced Coarse Golfer can add his own, such as damp matches for the inveterate pipe smoker. Or how about an umbrella which keeps collapsing? Or a towel for wiping the hands which leaves great shreds of lint everywhere?

Having dealt with items for lending, we must now consider the Coarse Golfer's own equipment.

First come the clubs. These should be the cheapest available and if they're second-hand so much the better. The inclusion of an old wooden-shafted club of strange design, purely for its effect on an opponent, is not a bad idea.

Never refer to clubs by their usual names, e.g. four iron and so forth, but by their archaic titles such as baffing-spoon, sand-iron, cleek, etc.

It doesn't matter a hoot if you get the name wrong. Nobody will be able to correct you. But the use of an archaic name will make an opponent respect you and give him a feeling that he's missed something in his golf education.

Stating 'I think I can just make the green with a cleek' may sometimes be better than actually making the green. If an opponent should point out that you've described four different clubs as baffing-irons, explain there is no modern equivalent.

'Alf Padgham's was more like a modern six iron. But Vardon's was like a present-day four. The great thing is whether they are suitable for baffing. And that depends on the lie of the ball.'

Confuse an opponent by giving him advice involving old names, for example, 'If I were you, old chap, I'd take a baffie to this one.'

With luck he won't admit he doesn't know what a baffie looks like but will wildly pull any club from his bag at random. If it's the wrong one, say nothing, but if he should accidentally pick the right club, gently explain that he has chosen a cleek by mistake.

Of course he can ignore the whole charade. But even if he tries to do so, you will have left a tiny seed of doubt sprouting at the back of his mind.

My friend Askew has invented a whole series of completely imaginary old clubs: Clout, Swiping-Iron, Zunge, Fashie, Burk, Stone-Iron and Bonker.

I'm quite used to seeing his opponents desperately pulling clubs out of their bags and asking pathetically, 'Is this the one you mean?' Askew in fact claims that he won the Spring Cup by suggesting to his rival that he used a Bogging-Iron for a vital shot.

Upon buying his clubs and equipment a Coarse Golfer will come into contact with the Great Golf Racket. This is a commercial conspiracy, sponsored by those who make money from supplying equipment, to convince golfers that the answer to it all is simply to keep on spending money.

Golfers, of course, are easy meat for this sort of thing, for we all become as little children once there's a club in our hands, and grown men who have waded through fire and slaughter without blenching, break into tears at missing a two-foot putt.

Mature, philosophical people, not given to easy emotion, will clutch frantically at any new talisman offered by the manufacturers, whether it be balls, clubs or socks. If some enterprising person advertised a pill that would enable the patient to putt accurately, he'd sell fifty thousand bottles straight away.

I once spent a wet afternoon going through some golf magazines and adding up the strokes that advertisers claimed could be saved by their equipment.

It started off with some shoes ('Worth a stroke a hole') and then came trolleys ('Will knock three strokes off your game') and balls ('Guaranteed to give more distance and accuracy'). By the time I'd finished the whole ghastly parade of gloves, umbrellas, glucose tablets and wrist-exercisers, not to mention clubs, it appeared possible to save twenty-three strokes by using the advertised equipment.

And all this was apart from more intangible claims, such as 'Makes putting a pleasure.' Whoever wrote *that* had obviously never played golf.

The biggest mistake that golfers make when buying clubs is to take advice from the man who's selling them. They seem to know within a shilling just how much you can't afford and then persuade you to spend it.

Professionals are less pressing than shops in their sales talk, because they know that like an undertaker they'll get you in the end. As long as you're around the club, a gentle hint here and there ('That putter's not doing you any good, sir') will ensure a regular income for the rest of their life. But for a professional there is only one brand of clubs that are any good, and by a remarkable coincidence he happens to sell them.

Avoid big stores like the plague. Ordinary humans

are helpless against their golf salesmen. I remember once going into a West End shop with the sole intention of buying one tee (I am rather mean about tees). The conversation went as follows:

'I'd like a cheap, plastic tee please. Mauve if possible.'

'Certainly, sir. Going out this afternoon?'

'Not really. Just practising driving.'

'Is your driving giving trouble, sir?'

'Among other things, yes.'

'Have you considered whether it might be the club?'

'Oh, I don't think so. They're a very decent bunch of people. Of course you get the odd black sheep in every club, but generally speaking . . .'

'No sir, I meant the driver.'

'You mean that when I miss the ball altogether it might be the fault of the club? I've been telling them that for years and they wouldn't believe me.'

'I'm afraid, sir, few golfers realise that nine times out of ten it's the club that makes a bad drive. Are you hooking or slicing?'

'Both. Sometimes at once. I also have a tendency to hit the ball vertically.'

'Just as I thought. The grip is obviously too thick. I think you'll find, sir, that its causing you to grip the club too much in the fingers instead of the palm. Now if you'd just like to take this club, sir, and hold it in your normal manner . . . that's right . . . hmmm, a most unusual grip if I may say so. You've obviously played a great deal of hockey in your time, sir . . . ha, ha . . . quite so, it wasn't really very funny . . . now look at your left hand, sir, and tell me if this club doesn't feel more comfortable and easier to grasp?'

'By George, you're right. It really is very comfortable . . . let me give it a swish . . . gosh, that would have gone dead straight . . . here, give me a practice ball . . . kerdoink . . . kerdoink . . . straight down the middle every time. . . . I see it all now . . . that's what's been wrong for the last ten years. . . . I'll have this straight away. Wrap it up.'

'If I may say so, sir, it would be inadvisable to have a driver from a different set to the other clubs. You see these clubs were specially designed by Gary Snead to be a self-contained set. Their whip is different from other clubs—you can see the photograph here of a club on the ten-thousand-dollar whip-testing machine.'

'All right. I'll take the driver now and buy the rest later.'

'I'm afraid, sir, that this is the last set in the shop. And they've stopped making them now, sir. They're too expensive for the average golfer, sir. People seem to want success on the cheap these days.'

I asked him how much a set was. He told me and I roared with laughter. Then I found he was serious. I decided to sell an insurance policy or two and take them all. No price is too high for success at golf. I was idly swishing a club as he wrapped them when he spoke again.

'I trust I'm not being personal, sir,' he said, handing

me every syllable as if it was a coin, 'but have you ever considered your—ah—posture?'

I truthfully replied that I hadn't.

'Ah,' he said, 'so few golfers realise how important it is. Bad posture leads to a bad stance and is so often due to wearing old-fashioned underwear. Now we have in stock some elasticated driving and putting underpants which really will improve your stance. If while you're waiting you'd care to step behind that curtain . . .'

The underpants looked like something designed for a person with incontinence. While I was trying them on he shouted through the curtain and sold me two pairs of socks, some putting gloves, an inflatable collar to keep the left elbow straight, a film on how to drive and a lightning conductor which you were supposed to stick on your trolley. In emergency you could thrust it against trolley-bus wires and light a cigarette. He forgot the tee.

I found some difficulty walking in the supporting underwear until the salesman pointed out I had it on backwards ('The large arrow should point to the rear, sir'). But then I was ready.

I tottered out with the parcels and hastened to my local course where I rushed on to the practice ground. Here I lovingly unwrapped the new driver. I also tried the inflatable collar on my elbow but all my veins started to bulge, so I threw it away.

Thanks to my underwear I felt a man for the first time in years. And as for the driver it looked good, it felt good and by gosh it was going to be good. I smote.

The steward told me later that he was dozing in his chair when the ball entered the open window and shattered the mirror behind him.

'I though I was back in the war,' he said. 'I woke up shouting "Take cover, Mother, the Jerries are coming".'

I persevered with the new clubs for six months. I have never sliced so badly in my life. The blasted things seemed to have a built-in slice, although I remembered later that the famous player who lent his name to them was notorious for a natural slice, and perhaps that was why. Also, the patent underwear was chafing. At the end of six months I couldn't stand it any more and took them to the club professional.

'These clubs have got their own slice,' I said. 'Can you sell them for me? Someone who hooks should pay a good price for this little lot.'

He laughed sycophantically.

'No wonder you're slicing with these,' he said, 'the grip is *too thin*. You need something with a thicker grip. Now as it happens I've got a set of those new Arnold Nicklaus clubs in stock, and if you'd like to try one ...'

But I had already fled.

A Coarse Golfer, therefore, should ignore any attempts to sell him fourteen clubs and extraneous paraphernalia such as wind indicators, lace panties for the woods, extending poles and so forth.

Basically he requires one club. For in Coarse Golf

how far the ball travels is nothing to do with the type of club used. The deciding factor is how the ball is hit. One of the greatest difficulties for the Coarse Golfer is that whereas his average distance with a three iron is 90 yards he occasionally sends an eight-iron shot 200 yards when trying to make a short chip.

Given this situation, there really isn't much point in worrying about the subtle difference between a three iron and a four wood.

Neither will the quality or cost of the clubs make any difference. The average pro could beat a Coarse Golfer using an umbrella. As my Uncle Walter used to say as he watched me drive, 'You could have done that shot just as well with a club from Woolworth's, my boy.'

An expensive bag full of clubs will not necessarily impress an opponent. He may well come to the conclusion that you're one of those pathetic people who try to buy proficiency at sport through expensive equipment, like a poor lover who purchases an expensive bed.

I say a Coarse Golfer needs only one club and that also includes for putting. A driver used with a short grip is the finest putter ever invented, although some prefer a five iron. But convention demands the use of more than one club and one must bow to it. Even then, the maximum number of clubs needed by a Coarse Golfer is four. These are:

Something made of wood. This need not be used, as some people can't hit the ball with woods, but it gives

Cut Down on Clubs!

EVER SINCE I BOUGHT THESE NEW CLUBS I'VE FOUND GOLF **HARD WORK.** MY TIMING MUST BE WRONG, MIKE!

NO, ALF, IT IS NOT YOUR TIMING BUT YOUR **NEW CLUBS.** YOU ARE **WEARING YOURSELF OUT** DRAGGING THEM AROUND!

DON'T BE A SLAVE TO CONVENTION. BY USING ONE CLUB FOR SEVERAL DIFFERENT SHOTS YOU CAN **ELIMINATE** THREE-QUARTERS OF THEM. FOR A LOW TRAJECTORY I FREQUENTLY DRIVE **WITH MY PUTTER...**

AND I FREQUENTLY **PUTT** WITH MY **DRIVER** BUT REMEMBER, ALF, **NEVER** USE YOUR DRIVER ON THE GREEN WHEN, YOU ARE WITHIN **SIGHT OF THE CLUBHOUSE!**

a bad impression if there are no woods in the bag.

Secondly, something made of iron for hitting the ball long distances (all all-purpose Coarse belter). Also useful for retrieving balls under bushes, in streams, etc., thanks to the long handle and graceful head.

Thirdly, another smaller iron for hitting the ball in the air. Especially useful for playing out of the middle of dense thickets and so forth, and for waving away clouds of gnats.

Fourthly, a putter. And if you can drive further with a putter than with a wood then by all means do.

All else is superfluous. These clubs should be decently stowed in a small bag, preferably with a green fee label from the Royal Birkdale carelessly tied round its neck.

Balls should be the cheapest available, since their life will be brief, if spectacular, and tees can usually be picked up en route round the course.

DRESS : One of the signs of the Coarse Golfer is that his clothes frequently represent a mixture of the different sports at which he has failed in his life. For years I used to play in old football boots, a hockey jersey and a cricket sweater. But only those who are good at sport can afford to pay no attention to dress.

The Coarse Golfer should aim at a well-worn, but shabby appearance, as if the victor of many a fourball. A meaningless badge on the bosom might help ('What's that? Royal Hammersmith, I think . . .'). A good test of clothes is this : does the secretary wonder whether to turn you off the course or to invite you to have a drink?

Don't under-estimate the importance of dress. It can, for instance, demoralise an opponent. It certainly demoralised me playing during a heatwave at the seaside one holiday.

As I was coming out of the locker room I met a man who'd just arrived. We arranged to go round together and I waited in the sun on the first tee until he was changed.

Then he came out. To my horror he was wearing nothing above the waist but a string vest. To make things worse he was covered all over in hair. He looked uncannily like a guest at the Chimps' Tea Party.

It was a rather snooty sort of club so after greeting him I hinted gently, 'I'm not sure that the secretary would approve of you going round in only a vest.'

He stuck his face close to mine.

'Listen, mate,' he said, 'I'm a docker, see? This is what I wear when I'm working and it's hot. And this is what I wear when I'm playing golf and it's hot. And this is what my mates also wear on the course back home. And if that old geezer peering from the clubhouse window don't like it he knows what he can do. And if you don't like it you know what you can do. Right?'

'Right,' I assented feebly.

So we set off, but worse was to come. Within ten minutes the man was being followed by a cloud of insects. It started with a few flies at the second hole, but then he went into a wood at the third and when he came out there was a long cloud of gnats pursuing him like a comet's tail.

It was terribly difficult playing against him. For one thing the constant droning of the insects put me off my stroke time and time again. Besides, one or two of them, finding they couldn't push through the throng that surrounded him, gave up and took it out on me so that eventually I, too, was putting with a cloud round my head.

Finally, I realised with dread that we were being followed by the club captain, who, judging from his comments when I parked my car in his space earlier, would not be given kindly to seeing people playing in their vests. There seemed only one thing to do : pretend I had no connection with the man I was playing against. This is not easy.

Three times I conceded holes so we wouldn't be seen together on the green and four times deliberately drove into the woods so I wouldn't be seen walking down the fairway with him. By this means I managed to keep up an impression to any observer that I was playing by myself but pressing hard on the man in front.

However, under the strain, my play went to pieces and not surprisingly I lost six and five. Mopping our brows we walked to the clubhouse and I suggested a drink. My opponent agreed at once, but instead of changing marched straight into the luxurious bar in his vest, followed by the usual cloud of insects, considerably swollen by recruits from all parts of the course.

'Spiked shoes not allowed in the bar, sir,'
he said firmly

There was nothing else to do but go in with him. The steward looked at us with contempt and then ordered *me* outside.

'Spiked shoes not allowed in the bar, sir,' he said firmly.

I never went there again.

But the most disturbing thing I have ever encountered in golfing clothes was when playing against an American airman who not only smoked a cigar while driving from the tee, but who wore a leather flying jacket with a naked woman painted on it. She wobbled when he breathed.

To make matters worse he used to talk about what he'd done to her, and what he was going to do to her, as you played your stroke.

'She sure is some woman,' you would hear him mutter as you addressed the ball, which immediately appeared to vibrate on the tee.

'Don't tell me English women aren't passionate,' he leered as I reached the top of the backswing.

'Only two hours more,' he used to say as you prepared for a vital putt, 'and I'll be right there.' And with that he slapped the naked figure and gave an obscene growl.

Askew suggests this should be taken further and one should deliberately paint a jacket with scenes that would distress an opponent, for example, a graveyard when playing someone in ill-health, or pound sterling signs against an opponent who is broke. But this may be going too far.

4

Beware of the Bull

'The ball no question makes of Ayes and Noes,
But Here or There as strikes the player goes.'

THE RUBAIYAT OF OMAR KHAYYAM

I once knew a man who had played golf for twenty-five years. He'd never had a lesson in his life but he had a fairly natural swing and played to a solid, belt-'em-down-the-middle fifteen. People in the club liked him and they made him captain one year. He was a happy man.

Happy, that is, until he went on holiday to Devon for a fortnight's golf.

The first day that he played he found himself shanking once or twice. This was immediately followed by a thunderstorm which flooded several greens, although the two events weren't connected. So finding himself at a loose end with the course unplayable he went to the club pro and asked for an hour's tuition to cure his shank.

The pro took him outside and told him to make a few shots with a five iron so he could spot the trouble.

59

My friend swung his normal natural swing, perhaps not one which would satisfy the purist, but at any rate it sent the ball about 170 yards. The pro looked solemn.

'Do that again,' he said, 'only this time try to imagine that you have a handkerchief tucked under your right armpit.'

A fortnight later my friend was still taking lessons and the pro was still taking money, only by now he had graduated to imagining he was pulling a bell rope with his arms as he swung. The shank had gone. It had been replaced by a violent, uncontrollable slice.

That was three years ago. I still see my friend occasionally, but he is a changed man, moody, morose and introverted, constantly talking about what is wrong with his swing to such an extent that most members avoid him. His handicap is 23. His slice has gone, but he now hooks savagely. When I last saw him he was obsessed with pretending that his head was attached to his left foot by a long piece of string whenever he drove.

I quote the story as a warning. There is nothing sadder than the fate of a man or woman who falls among golf coaches, until he is chained to a pro like a neurotic to a psychiatrist and with less hope of cure. I only wish this was an exaggeration but I have in front of me a golf magazine in which a writer recommends a golfer to visit his pro once a month 'to have his grip checked'. Or perhaps it was to have his cheque gripped. Anyway, the result's the same.

The most pathetic case of coaching neurosis I knew

was a chap who used to sit next to me at work. He had been going to a pro once a week for two years and still couldn't break a hundred. And then one day he came bounding into the office crying out that he had just had the most wonderful morning's golf.

No, he said, he hadn't broken a hundred. Actually he didn't break 110. But at the end of the round he noticed he had developed corns all over his hands. So he showed them to the pro.

The pro examined them wisely.

'That's a good sign,' he said at last. 'These corns are exactly where they ought to be if you are holding the club right.'

The fact is that if professionals' teaching worked they would be out of a job, in the same way that bookmakers would be bankrupt if the punters made a profit. Instead of which, most of them have reached the stage of buying a new car when the ashtrays on the old one are full up.

Perhaps I am biased because of an unfortunate experience.

After I had been playing golf for three years it became obvious that there was something radically wrong. Or perhaps several things.

For one thing I was the only man in the history of the game to have a square swing. I believe, too, that I may have been standing too close to the ball. At any rate, I severely injured myself by hitting my own foot with a club and had to be carried off the tee, moaning feebly.

'Why don't you go to a pro?' said my partner, and recommended a chap employed by a big London store.

The pro took me into a little room with a net at one end and invited me to strike a ball at it. Since the net was only six feet away I actually managed to hit it first time.

'Not much wrong with that, sir,' said the pro, looking at his watch. 'Try again.'

So I did it again and I hit the net again. And that was all I did for half an hour while the pro muttered, 'Not bad at all, just a little less backswing, sir, that's fine . . . that's fine.'

I paid him a guinea and came back the following week. This time the results were even better. I hit the centre of the net every time.

'We'll soon have you right, sir,' said the pro, pocketing some more money and fixing up another appointment.

This went on for six weeks, by which time there was a hole in the net. Then suddenly the pro shook me warmly by the hand.

'I can do nothing more for you, sir,' he said. 'You've got it all. All you need now is to go out on the course and practise.'

It didn't seem to me that I was doing anything differently from when I first entered the shop but I set forth confidently to put my all into practice against my old friend Askew.

After five holes it became evident that the pro had been slightly optimistic when he said I had got it all.

Or perhaps he meant something different by 'all'. As Askew said, either I hadn't got any of it or else I had got the lot.

I must say Askew was rather irritating, jeering 'I can teach you nothing more, sir,' as the ball screamed away into the river, and asking me if I would do better if I had my little net in front of me.

I returned to the store vowing vengeance and met the pro just as he was shaking hands with a happy-looking young man and saying, 'I can do nothing more for you, sir, you've got it all. Just go out on the course and put it into practice.'

'I expect you remember me,' I said, staring at him accusingly. He never flinched. He must have been used to this situation.

'Yes I do, sir,' he said. 'Tell me, did you take my advice and give up the game?'

There is one other type of professional with whom I have crossed swords and that is the dear-old-Sandy type, morose and foul-mouthed Scotsmen whose idea of tuition is to insult everybody.

Sandy's idea of instruction is to stand there and just grunt while the unhappy pupil talks himself into a nervous breakdown.

'Do you think I'm taking too much backswing?' asks the pupil in an effort to break the terrible silence.

Sandy utters a word that sounds like 'Borch' and could mean anything.

'And perhaps I'm moving the hips laterally too much?'

'Borch.'

'And maybe piccolo-ing at the top of the swing?'

'Borch.'

'Or perhaps it's my wind-up?'

'Borch.'

'Am I showing too much knuckle?'

'Borch.'

In desperation the pupil finally asks. 'Perhaps you'll tell me exactly what's wrong with this one,' and takes a swing.

'What was wrong with that, please?' he asks humbly.

'Everything,' bellows Sandy, snatching the club from his pupil's hands and in a flash sending the ball 250 yards. 'Now do it like that.'

The pupil, who didn't have a ghost of a chance to see what Sandy did, makes a feeble imitation and is rewarded by Sandy commenting, 'Och hell, man, this isna a game of —— hockey, ye know. Are ye paralysed or something?'

After which dear old Sandy stamps away muttering, not forgetting, however, to collect his money later.

Oddly enough, Sandy will be regarded in the clubhouse as a rather lovable person. 'Dear-old-Sandy,' they say, 'his bark's worse than his bite. He's got a heart of gold underneath it all.'

But there is one infallible method of dealing with the dear-old-Sandys of this world when they are abusing you. Insult them. They then collapse like a pricked balloon and reveal the hidden heart of gold.

Women golfers must be warned against taking lessons from the good-looking, dark young assistant professional. If the pupil is between 16 and 45 she will almost certainly find she is removed to a remote part of the course for her instruction.

What happens then is a ghastly let-down. Instead of flinging his pupil down in the bracken the young fool spends the instructional hour pouring out his life story, and his hopes, and telling how the pro has a down on him.

To make matters worse, club gossip will have given the poor lad a reputation as a positive rapist of the golf course and he wonders why women are eyeing him in a peculiar manner all the time. Life is hard for an assistant pro.

In fairness to professionals, it can be a heart-breaking job. My friend Askew, for instance, almost wrecked a pro's career.

After the fifth lesson the pro flung down his club and cried, 'I can't stand it any longer, I tell you! You're ruining my game. You've had such an effect on me that I'm doing everything your way now. It's uncanny. Please, please, sir, go away and learn from someone else.'

A Coarse Golfer, in fact, will probably find that the best tips he will receive will be obtained by watching his partners. I remember talking to a little Irishman with a handicap of four who had been a caddy in Ireland.

'I expect you learned a lot from watching the top-class players,' I said.

'Jeeze, no,' he replied. 'I didn't learn a thing from them. It was the bad ones that taught me everything I know. You could see what was wrong the minute they swung a club. They was like a lot of ruptured crabs.'

But if a Coarse Golfer's approach to coaching should be one of deep suspicion, his approach to books and instructional articles should be that of a man signing a hire purchase agreement.

At least a professional has got to be present to watch the result of his advice but the writer of an instructional article is safe in the knowledge that he doesn't have to be around when someone puts it all into practice, with the result that he can afford to say anything.

The best advice I've ever read was in Bill Cox's book, when he says that if you drive badly probably the club is to blame. Well, I knew all the time it wasn't me.

The most incredible hint I've ever read was in a golfing magazine where a writer suggested that a player should let out a snort as he drives. Not the ghastly, strangled shout of a Coarse Golfer as he sees his ball heading for a cyclist on the main road, but a deliberate, forceful snort as the club hits the ball.

A former Open champion was quoted as saying, 'Snorting adds ten yards to my drive.'

It this should be so (although the mind boggles at great honking noises resounding all over the course on Sunday morning), then I believe this makes 31 things that a player has to remember when he takes a swing at the ball.

Part from the absurdity of this sort of advice, the mind of a Coarse Golfer works differently from that of an ordinary player. While the normal golfer is concentrating on such things as left elbow, hips, balls of the feet, clubface, transfer of weight, cocking of wrists, etc., the Coarse Golfer's mind is a jumble of thoughts, simple golfing thoughts like 'I mustn't do another air shot', all mixed up with domestic matters about whether he left the bath water running or whether his wife's being unfaithful.

Nobody knows what goes on in the mind of a top-class pro as he swings. Perhaps a vast blank, perhaps just a large balloon with '50,000 dollars' in the middle of it.

But the mind of a Coarse Golfer is a terribly jumbled mass of thoughts which reach a crescendo as he swings :

'It doesn't feel right . . . too late to stop now . . . wish I could remember if I locked the front door . . . don't like the wife going down the tennis club too much . . . can't tell *me* the mixed doubles went on till midnight . . . wonder if it would straighten up if I shut the clubface at the last minute . . . by George ! I reckon it *is* that bloke at the tennis club . . . oh hell, in the ditch again . . . no, I definitely didn't lock the front door. . . .'

Obviously this is due to the Coarse Golfer's lack of concentration. But when world champions write of the necessity for a sort of trance-like ecstasy as you swing, they forget that all they have to concentrate on is shutting out the noise of the helicopters and the whirring of cameras.

What would Arnold Palmer do if he had the experience that befell me on the first tee at Moor Park when as I started my downswing my partner said loudly, 'My wife has refused to sleep with me?'

I think it typifies the Coarse Golfer's attitude to the game that although the ball was still somewhere around my heel I exclaimed, 'Not again, old chap. Why don't you go to the Marriage Guidance Council?'

One reason why I distrust written advice about golf is that I know something of how part of it comes into print. The first thing to remember is that if a man's earning 300,000 dollars a year he is not going to waste his time writing articles for the *Golfer's Friend* at twenty guineas a time, apart from the fact that he is probably only just able to sign his name on a cheque.

In the days of the old *News Chronicle* Sports Room Open Tournament, I used to partner a chap called Fred who ghosted a weekly article for a famous golfer. The two had never met. The champion had not only never read one of his own articles, he didn't even know who wrote them. That was just as well since Fred's golf had to be seen to be believed.

But that didn't stop Fred, whose idea of a good round was when he only lost three balls, sending out each week a stream of advice couched in the most pedantic manner possible ('After five years of winning every major golf award I can state categorically that anyone can become a scratch golfer if he can learn to keep his head down').

I used to quote pieces at Fred as he played his seventh shot from behind a bush.

Then one week Fred made a very simple mistake. He got left mixed up with right, and wrote something about what to do with the left arm when all the time he meant the right arm. I tried it out and followed literally it would have resulted in the player strangling himself with his elbows on the follow-through.

Fred sat back and waited for the letters of complaint. They came all right, but not in the form expected. The first one read something like this :

Dear Sir,

While trying to put your advice on getting extra length into practice on the first tee at Sunningdale yesterday, I am afraid that I dislocated my shoulder. I would be most grateful if you could spare time from your busy life to tell me what I am doing wrong. I enclose a stamped, addressed envelope for reply.

The other three hundred were nearly all like that, humble, pathetic letters from men who had strained themselves, injured themselves, wasted whole days practising and just wanted to know what they were doing wrong.

There was one exception to the correspondence. One reader wrote to say he had put the advice into practice and as a result had knocked ten strokes off his game.

Fred was so affected by all this that he refused to publish a correction. Instead the affair went to his head and he began to write outrageous advice, odd hints he remembered from his father, little tips he always found useful such as shutting his eyes when he putted, and so on.

Fortunately for the game of golf, six months later the Great Man whose name was over the article saw a player making an incredible swing and nearly strangling himself. When asked why he swung like that the man replied, 'I got the idea from one of your articles.'

The Great Man had the article spelled out for him by his literary agent and simply commented, 'Fire that bum.' And so they did. But the articles were never as interesting afterwards.

So next time you're worried about what's wrong with your forward press, just remember what W. G. Grace said when asked for the secret of how to play cricket.

'Put bat to ball,' said the doctor.

5

Perils of the First Tee

'The driving is like the driving of Jehu, the
son of Nimshi; for he driveth furiously.'

THE BOOK OF KINGS

Like all Coarse Sport, golf is best enjoyed in fantasy.
No one believes that a bald-headed wreck in the seventh
team of some obscure London old boys' rugby club
really enjoys spending his Saturday afternoons limping
around a swamp. What he really enjoys is slaking his
thirst after the game and talking about great matches
of the past from the comfort of an armchair.

So it is with Coarse Golf. The past games take on an
aura of pleasure and one forgets the time when you tried
to snap your putter, the pitiful feeling of futility about
it all. All that is remembered is the shot when
everything went right. The conviction grows that the
two holes you did decently were your normal game, and
the other sixteen just an unfortunate aberration.

I always think that the Coarse Golfers who get
most out of the game are those who have been com-

pelled to give it up, or those who are always going to have a round next week.

The height of fantasy golf is Postal Golf. This was invented by Askew and myself for use during the depths of winter but some people might prefer it to the ordinary game even when the weather is good.

The rules are simple. A course is selected and each player has a card. The player who has the honour goes into his garden and drives a plastic practice ball, and on the basis of the stroke makes an estimation of what would have happened to the ball.

He then sends a postcard to his opponent, saying for instance, HAVE JUST DRIVEN TWO HUNDRED YARDS BUT SLICED INTO ROUGH GRASS ON FIRST.

His opponent replies, and then both go on to their irons. Putting is done in the dining room, using a tumbler on the carpet.

This harmless and amusing game was, however, wrecked by the sheer egotism of Askew. While I honestly recorded each slice, hook or dunch (the penalty for slicing or hooking was the compulsory use of an eight iron for the next shot, with subsequent loss of distance), Askew's overweening sense of his own importance led him to make fantastic claims.

It all began with a postcard reading: HAVE JUST HIT THREE HUNDRED YARD DRIVE STRAIGHT DOWN MIDDLE.

When I replied: HAVE LANDED TWO FEET FROM PIN WITH THREE IRON, Askew started claiming a succession of birdies, first lulling me into a false sense of security by admitting that he was in a bunker and then claiming to have sunk the bunker shot.

We finally abandoned the game when, after I had clearly won a hole, he sent a postcard: YOU ARE PENALISED TWO STROKES BECAUSE YOUR BALL STRUCK MINE ON THE GREEN.

We did not talk to each other for some time after that but I still think the game could be successful, provided it is not played between two psychopaths.

But however much the Coarse Golfer likes to indulge in fantasy the time must come when he has to face up to reality and march out on to the course.

The initial problem that will confront him is the first tee.

Driving from the first tee can be an ordeal even for a good player. For a Coarse Golfer it is a terrifying experience. This is partly because one's efforts are usually watched by a large gallery impatiently swishing their drivers.

It is some comfort, though, that those who do the most swishing while waiting invariably drive the worst (Law Six of Coarse Golf: 'He who swisheth most driveth least').

When one is called to take the stroke, the arms, never fully under control, become like ramrods, the clubhead is seized with a life of its own, the hips lock and the wrists have all the strength and flexibility of a couple of overripe bananas.

In my own case, whenever I drive from the first tee, my left foot always twitches off the ground on the backswing, so I am left standing on one leg. This is quite uncontrollable, and short of spiking the foot to the floor I don't know what can be done.

The reason for this sort of thing is not only the fear of appearing a fool in front of the gallery, but also the First Tee Syndrome, an unreasonable fear that the patient will be thrown off golf courses. It can be very persistent and while it can be alleviated cannot be cured completely.

The fear is not entirely without basis as far as I am concerned. I was ejected from a golf course after my very first stroke in the game.

I had been hacking around secretly for some time with my old wooden-shafted clubs, when a friend suggested that the moment had come for me to spread my wings on a real course and he unwisely arranged to play the next Sunday morning.

There was a long queue behind us as I teed up in front of the clubhouse. Completely unnerved I took my courage in both hands, decided to cut out the address and struck savagely at the ball with the laudable intention of getting away from this lot as soon as possible.

A huge clod of earth vanished down the fairway and behind me came a low moan.

Again I swung desperately and this time came a satisfying click and a small dot hurtled towards the hole. It was the clubhead followed by what seemed a hundred yards of twine.

At the same time a man standing about fifty yards away gave a great shout, flung up his arms and fell senseless to the ground. I started to move towards the stricken man when my partner, who was a solicitor, stepped forward and put a hand on my arm.

'Say nothing, old chap,' he muttered. 'You are not obliged to make a statement and don't apologise in case that should be construed as an admission of liability.'

'I'm not making a statement,' I explained. 'I want to retrieve the ball. It's the only new one I've got.'

There was, however, no sign of the ball except for the words 'Dunlop 65' imprinted upside down on the forehead of the club bore, who was being helped into the bar by his friends.

My attempts at apologising without admitting liability ('I deeply regret the injury you appear to have suffered from some unknown person') merely resulted in a torrent of abuse and I returned to the tee. It seemed the only thing to do.

As I swung for my third attempt there was no gallery. The waiting players had all retreated to the verandah, and some to the bar, where their faces were pressed against the window. But before I could strike the ball the club secretary came running across to the tee.

'Leave the course immediately, sir,' he bellowed. 'The steward will refund your green fee.'

'I'm sorry,' I muttered humbly. 'I didn't mean to hit that man on the head. It was an accident.'

'I don't know what the devil you're talking about,' said the secretary, 'but I will not tolerate people who *wheel their trolleys over the tee.*'

I mention this to show that there are more hazards on a first tee than hitting the ball in all directions. Perhaps one day golf clubs will see reason and provide a first tee which is heavily boxed in with soundproof material, so that all spectators will see is the ball trickling feebly forth.

However, there is nothing that the Coarse Golfer can do but take the tee as he finds it, even though it will probably be rather different when he leaves it, having gained several deep indentations.

One of the essential precautions to take upon driving from the first tee is to make sure that you are on the right course and playing with the correct opponents.

This may seem rather obvious but I give the advice following an unfortunate incident last year when a complete stranger turned up for a meeting of the Warreners' Golf Society at West Herts and said he was a friend of Peter Brown who had asked him to play in his place.

'How thoughtful,' we said, 'good old Pete.'

The stranger played a superb morning round, which looked as if it would win the cup.

At lunch we asked what was wrong with Peter.

'His old trouble,' said the stranger. 'Still, you've got to expect it at his age. We're lucky to have him still with us.'

Since Peter was a virile twenty-two-year-old we pressed for further information as a result of which it turned out the stranger was a friend of a totally different Peter Brown and he was supposed to be playing on the *East* Herts course. He left hurriedly in a taxi and we never saw him again.

When driving from the first tee, a Coarse Golfer should also make absolutely sure that he is playing to the correct green. I have rarely known anything as embarrassing as when myself and a friend found after making our drives that we had played to the eighteenth. Fortunately our drives were so inaccurate that we were able to use them for the proper hole.

A Coarse Golfer would probably prefer to use an iron off the first tee. He certainly ought to use an iron off every tee. Any Coarse Golfer could knock ten strokes off his game by taking a six iron off every tee and trying to hit the ball straight for a hundred yards, instead of swishing wildly with a driver and sending the ball underneath his trolley.

However, it is not considered good golf to use an iron on a long hole, although I suspect this idea is spread by the club manufacturers. Therefore, some sort of excuse must be made. Here are some suggestions :

'They say Palmer never touches his woods now.'

'The pro said he hadn't sold a wood for six months.'

'An old golfer told me I had the finest iron action he had ever seen.'

'You don't need woods on a piddling little course like this.'

'The doctor took one look at my wrist and said: "No more woods until that tendon's cleared up".'

'Funny, you won't believe this, but I meant to play a wood and absent-mindedly took out a three iron.'

77

(To be used after the stroke only.)

Feeble though these excuses are, they at least give some sort of protection.

Strange how using an iron for a long hole is considered such a sin in golf, and it is typical of how the game upsets normal, civilised values.

The biggest crook in town can be popular in a golf club provided he pays for his round of drinks. But if Dr. Barnardo himself used an iron off the first tee people would start whispering in corners of the bar, 'He's not a bad chap but there's something sinister about him. Never uses his woods y'know.'

A friend, Mr. Tony Owen, of Ealing, tells me he ruined his health through taking a three iron off the first tee at St. Andrews.

'It was the silence that got me down,' he said. 'Nobody said a word. But ever since then I've slept badly. I wake up after a nightmare, and I can still see them all staring at me, just standing there *staring*.'

In all this I have made no reference to caddies. A Coarse Golfer will not normally have any connection with these people.

I can say with perfect honesty that I had been playing golf for fifteen years before I saw my first caddy.

This event took place at Royal Wimbledon when I was playing in a society match. As my partner and I stood on the first tee I noticed a crowd of men eyeing us in a curious way and I whispered to my partner, 'Who are those shabbily dressed people crowding

Wreck Those Drives!

round the tee? Shall I tell them the Labour Exchange is further down the road?'

'Those are caddies,' replied my partner stiffly. 'Haven't you ever seen one before?'

It then came to me that I hadn't—they don't have them in the sort of places where I usually play golf— and I favoured them with a good stare, which was returned with interest, rather insolently I thought.

As luck would have it, my drive was slightly sliced. Not to put too fine a point on it, it vanished off the toe of the club with a low humming sound and scattered the caddies in all directions. No one spoke. They all reassembled as if nothing had happened and simply looked at me with rheumy eyes.

It was one of the most terrifying experiences of my life (even worse than when our television set caught fire), and I made up my mind there and then that I would never have the courage to employ a caddy, even if I had the money.

But to return to the tee itself. It is in the interests of all Coarse Golfers that they should leave the first tee as quickly and with as little fuss as possible.*

For this reason no attempt should be made to interfere with an opponent's play on the first hole, for example by using the Sweets of Damocles. Both players should concentrate on getting as far away from the clubhouse as possible, as quickly as possible.

Only then may battle start in earnest.

*In an effort to do this Askew once threw the ball off the tee.

6

Tactics

'Oh the dirty little pill
Went rolling down the hill
And rolled right into a bunker.
From there to the green
I took thirteen
And then by God I sunk her.'

TRAD.

To be a successful Coarse Golfer one must realise that all the virtues of golf are those attributes which civilised society rightly scorns, e.g. playing for one's self, introversion, fanaticism, brooding, taciturnity, obsession with figures and so forth.

The Coarse Golfer is therefore perfectly entitled to adopt what methods he can to survive, and win if possible.

The great divergence between ordinary golf and Coarse Golf is that the ordinary golfer will attempt to beat his opponent by taking fewer strokes. This is out of the question for a Coarse Golfer. His only hope of achieving anything lies in persuading his opponent to take more strokes than himself.

In Coarse Golf it is also a victory if an opponent wins without getting any satisfaction from doing so. Thus another definition of Coarse Golf might be: 'The art of winning without taking fewer strokes.'

The secret of successful Coarse Golf is to arouse emotion in the opponent.

Emotion is the curse of the bad golfer. The reason why Coarse Golfers are what they are is not because they are physically incapable of hitting a ball straight —any fool can do that—but because they are *emotionally* incapable of it.

After all, if a golfer can do one good stroke there's no reason why he shouldn't follow it up with another. But a Coarse Golfer never puts two good shots together for the simple reason that if he does make a good one he's bubbling over with glee about it and tries to hit the cover off the ball.

Having made a bad shot the Coarse Golfer swings to the other extreme and approaches the next with his tiny mind a jumble of little scraps of misinformation as he swings ('I think that paper-back book said cock the wrists earlier, but the *Golf World* article said you shouldn't worry about that . . .').

Here's proof of the effect of emotion. The finest game of golf I have ever seen in my life was played by a friend who met me at lunch with the news that he was bankrupt. His one-man business had collapsed.

The tragedy stunned him so much that he had become emotionally quite numb. As a result he went round in twelve strokes under his handicap.

'I am a ruined man,' he groaned as he drove 250 yards from the first tee.

'My God, whatever will happen to the wife and kids?' he muttered as he sank a twelve-foot putt.

'I shall never survive the shock,' he mumbled as he chipped straight down from thirty yards.

I don't think he even realised he had won six and five; he just tottered into the clubhouse with a glassy stare on his face and buried his head in his hands. Yet when I played him again three months later, with all his worries solved by a last-minute take-over, his golf was as bad as business was good.

'They've promised me seven thousand a year and a seat on the board of the parent company,' he said as he sent the ball flying into a pond.

'Later I'll probably get a five per cent commission on increased turnover,' he warbled, digging out several pounds of earth from the tee.

'There's talk of sending me to America for six months,' he chirped, hitting the ball straight between his legs.

It is not necessary to arouse a particular emotion in an opponent's bosom. Any one will do.

Nature has provided us with a wide range, from fear, envy, grief, lust and rage to joy, happiness and unspeakable pleasure. From a golf point of view it doesn't matter which is chosen, but obviously anger is a good choice. I defy anyone to drive well when they are in a paroxysm of rage.

Politics are an excellent way of arousing rage. A few

well-chosen questions in the locker room will reveal an opponent's political sympathies.

It would be too crude to say in the middle of an opponent's swing: 'In my opinion the Leader of the Opposition is a half-witted pig.'

However, I see no reason why in casual conversation on the tee one should not remark airily, 'I must say I thought the Chancellor of the Exchequer acted extremely courageously in putting up income tax. The trouble with this country is that we've all got too much money to spend.'

Signs that any shafts have gone home will be a twitching of the jaw muscles, a flushing of the cheeks and an attempt to hit the ball 400 yards.

Lust is an extremely useful emotion to arouse. Draw the attention of an opponent to any attractive women golfers nearby and expound at length upon the sensual pleasures of their shapely forms.

Sympathy is one of the best emotions, because once an opponent feels it would be unfair if he won the game the battle is half over.

Askew's normal way of achieving this is to fall into a deep reverie while addressing the ball and to stare fixedly at the ground.

He then heaves a Hamlet-type sigh, comes to with a start, and says, 'I'm sorry about that, old chap. I was just thinking how in the midst of life we are in death, as the Good Book has it.'

He gives no further explanation except perhaps to say what the Good Book is, if an opponent should think he means the Rules of Golf.

Another of his ingenious alternatives is to add, 'Funny how one gets attached to animals, isn't it? I mean they twine their little paws around your heart

Lust is an extremely useful emotion to arouse

with their funny ways. You know, I can see him standing there now with his tail wagging and those trusting eyes looking up at me. I should never have let him off the lead. Ah well, better get on with the game I suppose. Life is for the living.'

This actually reduced one opponent to tears.

'Keep thinking of that little dog of yours,' he said apologetically, wiping his eyes. 'I had one like that. Then one day we left the front gate open and he ran away. But the wife always leaves the gate open for him to come back. We know that one day we'll hear his little paws pattering up the path.'

Unfortunately this sad story so affected Askew that the round had to be abandoned, as both players were blubbering into their handkerchiefs.

Remember that attempts to arouse sympathy will only work with strangers.

I had an embarrassing experience playing against the B.B.C. in a society game, when I forgot that one of my opponents had played against me two years before.

This time I was using ill-health as my weapon, and kept clutching my breast, wincing, and remarking bravely, 'Don't worry about me. The doc says I might go on for years.'

I looked round for sympathy but my opponent merely remarked, 'Well, you're entitled to have a stroke on this hole in any case.'

Later he commented, 'You seem to have a lot of bad luck, don't you? Last time we played your wife had run off with your best friend, the cat had died and the doctor had given you six months to live.'

A situation like that is hopeless, and the wise Coarse Golfer will admit defeat, although in this instance I was able to retrieve matters a little by surreptitiously tying a black armband to my jacket in the changing room.

Do not forget the importance of getting in several good blows on the tee. Remember that as a general rule the only places where two Coarse Golfers meet are the tee and the green. A player who leaves all his wheezes to the fairway may never have a chance to apply them.

An opponent is also at his most vulnerable on the tee, especially after his drive, which gives a wonderful opportunity for stirring up the dreaded emotion. This can be done whether the drive was successful or not.

After his opponent has struck the ball (or failed to do so), there are only two comments that need to be made by the Coarse Golfer. These are :

'Hard luck !'

'Good shot !'

Any other comment is superfluous.

These two phrases should be used in reverse of their correct usage. In other words, a bad stroke should be greeted with 'Good shot !' and a good shot with the comment, 'Hard luck !'

The simplest way to explain this apparent paradox is by two practical examples.

Practical Example No. 1. An opponent hits a good, straight drive two hundred yards down the centre of the fairway. Having done so, he corrects his grip, adjusts his follow-through, and then stands like a statue, staring towards the green with an expression of intense pain on his face, which he imagines indicates immense concentration.

Make no mistake, he is waiting for someone to say how good he is.

'Hard luck !' says the Coarse Golfer.

The striker's arms drop a little and he lowers his club slightly, but still keeps up his ridiculous pose as he replies testily, 'How do you mean, hard luck ?'

'I think you may be among all that wretched clover. They shouldn't let it grow on the fairway. It clings at the clubhead terribly.'

Whether your opponent believes this or not doesn't matter. It is the effect on the next stroke which counts. And when he walks down the fairway and finds his ball sitting up nicely in the mown grass he will be extremely annoyed.

'All that clover indeed,' he will mutter as he prepares to address the ball. 'There isn't any within miles. The bloke must be blind. Clover indeed! *I'll show him.*'

I have italicised the last sentence because that is the key to the success of this little plan. When a golfer says to himself, 'I'll show him,' he is doomed.

This is summed up in Law Seventy-three of Coarse Golf: 'When a player is aroused so that he feels it is necessary for him to demonstrate to an opponent his superiority, then that player will forfeit the hole.'

The most likely practical effect will be for the man who mutters 'I'll show him' to strike the ground a foot behind the ball. With luck he will sprain his wrist as well.

Personally, I always punch at the ball viciously, with no suggestion of a swing, and bombard people on the next fairway.

Practical Example No. 2. We now consider a bad drive by an opponent. Let us say, for example, that he tops the ball abominably, so that it scarcely has the strength to reach the edge of the tee.

'Good shot,' says the Coarse Golfer firmly.

His opponent turns round in utter disbelief.

'Are you out of your mind?' he says, pointing to the ball which is nestling happily near the tee-box. 'It may be a good shot by your miserable standards but not by mine.'

The Coarse Golfer looks surprised and peers into the distance.

'I thought it would be down the fairway judging by the way you hit it,' he replies. 'You gave it enough force to reach the cross-bunkers at least. Are you sure that's your ball?'

'Of course I'm —— well sure, you fool.'

'Would you like me to take a look? Sometimes they drive across here from the thirteenth, you know. I mean, it's not really likely that you only got that far, is it? You were telling me only the other day how much your driving had improved.'

That is enough. Any man who is not by this time filled with a great desire to beat his opponent about the head with his club is not human. This suppressed hostility will, however, not be directed against the Coarse Golfer but against the ball on the next stroke, with inevitable and fearful results.

But note that it is possible to go too far. Askew once goaded an opponent into such desperation that he seized Askew by the coat and threatened him with serious injury if he ever spoke again on the tee.

For the rest of the round Askew kept repeating, 'I

shall say nothing', until he nearly drove his opponent insane.

I must mention that my Uncle Walter, although firmly holding to the 'arouse emotion' theory, believes that it is more subtle to arouse joy rather than rage in the bosom of the opposition.

Who can resist the serpent-like tongue of the flatterer?

Thus after a good drive by an opponent he apparently cannot conceal his joy, burbling happily all the way along the fairway, 'I must say, old chap, I haven't seen a finer drive in years. You young fellows really know how to hit the ball. I can see you don't have to worry about getting your swing right. All you've got to do now is to get an eight iron, *belt it pretty hard,* and you're there.'

The key phrase, italicised, is 'belt it pretty hard'.

Who can resist the serpent-like tongue of the flatterer? There really are only two choices—to belt it hard or to make a great effort not to belt it hard.

Either way the result will be the same.

But if it is important to arouse emotion in an opponent it is equally important to suppress your own feelings completely.

Upon playing his stroke the Coarse Golfer must show no outward emotion at all. No comment should be allowed, whether bad or good. Even to show pleasure can be dangerous.

One of the greatest mistakes I have ever made in golf came at the old first hole at Coombe Wood in 1959, when I was playing in the *News Chronicle* competition against Ian Wooldridge, who knew nothing of my golf and was rather apprehensive.

My drive swirled off the fairway, vanished into the wood on the left, struck a tree and bounced back on to the fairway about seventy yards in front of the tee.

I was so pleased that I danced about the tee, waving my driver and shouting, 'I've cracked the game. A 70-yarder straight down the middle!'

As Ian said afterwards, 'When you're playing a man who thinks he's cracked the game when he drives 70 yards via an old beech tree you've got him on toast.'

Neither should rage or annoyance be shown over a bad drive. Nothing encourages an opponent more than to see you gibbering with anger and calling upon strange gods.

Apart from anything else this can have peculiar results. I remember taking tea with my cousin's wife in Camberley one afternoon when my cousin Arthur came in from the course. Normally Arthur is a placid man, a good husband and father, liked by all, but on this occasion he looked like Hamlet climbing out of Ophelia's grave.

'Did you lose, Arthur?' asked his wife tenderly.

'Yes,' said Arthur. 'I lost the game, five bob and my number two wood.'

There was a moment's pregnant silence.

'How do you *lose* a number two wood?' asked his wife.

'It's quite easy,' said Arthur, 'you throw it away.'

With that he seized a cup of tea and began to gibber into it.

When he had recovered himself we pieced together the story. It appeared that after driving badly throughout the game he made a particularly bad shot on one of the later holes, whereupon he whirled his driver round his head three times, like Excalibur, and hurled it into a wood.

Unfortunately, no arm clothed in white samite, mystic, wonderful, appeared to grasp the club. It simply vanished among the trees.

Arthur immediately repented of his folly and went to look for it but there was no trace.

Later that evening they organised a family search in the dark with torches. It took three-quarters of an hours and then someone shone his torch upwards and saw the club hanging in the branches like a dead Red Indian.

Let that be a warning of the perils of emotion.

7

Fern Grot and God Wot

'O'er rough and smooth she trips along
And never looks behind.'

WORDSWORTH

Watching a Coarse Golf party split up after their
strokes is like sitting in the stalls at a Shakesperian
history, when the King despatches his Lords to meet
the rebels.

'And thou good brother Warwick take the North
While our fair cousin Gloucester guards the South
And Essex hies himself unto the East
While we ourselves do hold the stormy West. . . .'

Normally all players will march in opposite directions. It is not unknown for some to march forwards
and others backwards if, for instance, a shot has re-
bounded from a shelter.

Yet because a Coarse Golfer spends so much time in
the rough he does have an opportunity for experiences which never come the way of better men. To

93

him a golf course does not consist of a series of tees and greens linked by well-mown fairways, but of dense stretches of jungle. The Coarse Golfer wanders on the long summer afternoons through fern grot, rose plot and God wot. He knews the scent of the ragwort (whatever that is), the song of the plover, and the sweet, cloying smell of decaying dead animals.

He knows, too, the meandering little streams which wind their way through the woods and probably has invented his own names for some of nature's features, titles such as 'Calamity Spinney', 'Three-stroke Wood' and 'Bastard Bushes'.

It is a strange sub-world, this life in the rough, and one which the better golfers miss. I sometimes feel sorry for a good golfer who can go round one of the most beautiful stretches of countryside in the world without ever leaving the deadly dull stretch of flat grass which comprises the fairway.

Only the other week I watched two women golfers put their shots into a wood and vanish after them.

'Women golfers,' I sneered, and struck a firm, masculine stroke. The ball feebly dribbled into the same wood.

When I went in there to search for it I found the women on their knees gathering flowers and chirping to each other like birds.

'You always get such lovely primroses here,' one of them told me, 'but I think the bluebells in the wood by the seventeenth are nicer.'

Incidentally, it was a fascinating experience following these women round the course (I couldn't go through—I tried twice but kept putting the ball on the next fairway).

Half the time they picked a club simply because they liked the colour of the grip.

'Not that big club, Daphers,' said the older woman. 'Take the one with the pretty blue handle. It goes with your skirt.' And they seemed completely impervious to all the normal emotions of golf.

If they muffed a drive they didn't dance all over the tee in rage like any civilised human being but started worrying whether their cap was on straight. Getting into trouble didn't worry them at all, they seemed to regard the ball as a kindly guide leading them to interesting parts of the countryside.

In fact, when young Daphers put her ball straight into the foulest morass in the south of England she positively jumped for joy and screamed, 'Oh, I'm so glad it's gone there, we can see if those blackbirds have hatched out yet.'

But then that's women's golf all over. Don't believe that they are more emotional than men. It's the male who gets hysterical over that little white ball, it's the man who bursts into tears over his putts. Women don't really care—as long as their hair's not coming adrift.

But to return to the rough. One of the blessings of being a Coarse Golfer is the interesting things that happen in there.

Indeed, my friend Askew married a woman he met in the rough. At the height of summer he sliced a shot into a stretch of gorse and bushes and on going to search for the ball came upon a young woman in a deep sleep with the ball resting six inches from her head.

Askew immediately claimed that the girl counted as a loose impediment and he was entitled to brush her away. I countered this by pointing out that loose impediments, according to the rules, included 'dung, worms and insects, and casts or heaps made by them', and she didn't come into that category.

'In that case,' said Askew, 'she is young growth and I shall move two club lengths away.'

All might yet have been well but Askew is not at his best in a difficult lie and the girl was awoken, not by the sound of club hitting ball, but by the monotonous repetition of an obscene word, varied by occasional crackling of the undergrowth.

Her first reaction was to give a shrill scream, to which Askew replied that he could well understand her being upset at seeing the rotten lie he was in, but not to worry, he had only taken five so far and there was still a chance of doing the hole in single figures if everyone would please keep quiet.

They got married six months later, and now have been blessed with a daughter and a son whose real name I never know because Askew insists on referring to him as 'Young Casual Water'.

For some time after the wedding Askew always used to doff his cap before he drove from the third, but nowadays I notice that he is merely inclined to mutter something under this breath.

However, most of the time a Coarse Golfer spends in the rough will be taken up more prosaically searching for lost balls.

It is extremely important for a player to find his own ball first. This will enable him to cross to the other side of the fairway to help his opponent, and by sneaking up behind him you may well find him improving his lie, if not worse. A quiet cough in the middle of his vile deed is sufficient.

In a previous chapter I have criticised coaching methods, but one piece of coaching well worth while would be lessons from a professional deerstalker or Red Indian on the art of sneaking quietly about the rough. It would repay the trouble a thousandfold.

I am, of course, assuming there are no caddies and I wouldn't know what to suggest if there were any since I have never spoken to a caddy in my life.

However, I understand that there is a golf club in Surrey where it is tacitly agreed that on starting a game the player hands the caddy several replicas of his ball for use in emergencies. A friend who has played there assures me that if you don't the caddy asks you for them, accompanying his request with nods and winks and suggestive jerks of the head.

Upon the discovery of an opponent's ball it is best to try and remain for his stroke, if possible. Left to himself he will almost certainly bend the rules of golf, if not actually break them.

Askew, for instance, says anything under two hundred years old is young growth, and claims the right to drop two club lengths away.

'Young growth is a comparative term,' said Askew when I found him moving his ball from beside an aged oak that might well have sheltered Robin Hood in its day. 'Compared with that elm over there, this tree is a mere infant.'

Good heavens, Askew once tried to claim that the North Sea was casual water.

Playing on the East Coast he struck his ball into a tidal creek, and to my astonishment waded in and retrieved it, saying, 'They ought to be ashamed of themselves, leaving all that damn casual water all over the fairway. I'll drop without penalty.'

But assuming you are able to dicover an opponent's ball along with him, what can be done when he immediately :

(*a*) Flattens the grass for a yard around 'to identify the ball as I'm entitled to do'.

(*b*) Lifts the ball to make doubly sure and replaces it on a tiny mound.

(*c*) Moves several hundredweight of sundry twigs, leaves, branches, etc., from behind and in front of the ball.

(*d*) Destroys two or three bushes, and when unable to move a particularly strong sapling asks you to bend it down so he can play over it.

(*e*) Waggles the clubhead around so as to create a clear space around the ball.

(*f*) Treads down a tump behind the ball.

Watch Your Opponent

"NO MATTER HOW WELL I PLAY, MIKE, MY OPPONENT ALWAYS TAKES **FEWER STROKES** THAN ME. WHAT IS WRONG WITH MY GOLF?"

"**NOTHING** IS WRONG WITH YOUR GOLF, ALF. YOUR OPPONENT IS PROBABLY **A CHEAT!** LET ME GO ROUND WITH YOU NEXT TIME!"

"HA-HA! ALF IS ON THE OTHER SIDE OF THE FAIRWAY. HE NEED **NEVER KNOW** ABOUT THIS!"

ALFS OPPONENT

"WHAT A PITY! YOU HAVE TO CONCEDE **TWO STROKES** FOR LIFTING OUT! AND ANOTHER **TWO PENALTY STROKES** FOR IMPROVING YOUR LIE!"

GASP!

MIKE INTERVENES!

"REMEMBER, ALF, IN **COARSE GOLF** THE IMPORTANT THING IS NOT HOW **YOU** PLAY, BUT HOW YOUR **OPPONENT** PLAYS.

IF HE IS WINNING CONSISTENTLY THEN EITHER HE IS **CHEATING** — OR YOU **ARE NOT CHEATING** ENOUGH!"

SEETHE SEETHE SEETHE

Remember it is absolutely useless appealing to the Rules of Golf.

Firstly, it is doubtful whether you will know them, or even understand them if you do.

Secondly, the opponent will deny that the rule applies on this occasion, even if shown it in black and white.

Thirdly, to resort to the rules lays you open to a strict interpretation. Your opponent may well say that if you are going to play strict rules of golf, then what about that time you took your drive again because 'We never count air shots on the first tee'?

After all, life as a Coarse Golfer would be impossible without those little concessions we extend to each other such as starting a hole again if both players' drives land in the ditch or holding back branches that interfere with an opponent's swing. It's only when such concessions are abused that action must be taken.

Worse still, he may well unearth some obscure rule, and say that if you are going to be finicky then he is going to claim the hole because you spoke to that old chap by the tee and Rule 9 specifically forbids a player to seek advice from an outside agency.

No, the only result of appealing to the Rules of Golf will be to give your opponent an incalculable moral advantage as he waxes righteous about your past misdeeds until finally you are apologising for mentioning the matter.

The best technique is to invent an imaginary rule

and then make a great show of *allowing your opponent to break it.*

It is only human nature that a golfer accused of breaking the well-known rules will deny it. But there is no disgrace attached to breaking an obscure rule inadvertently, and your opponent may admit to this, if you allow him to proceed notwithstanding.

Say nothing as an opponent flattens the grass and asks you to hold back some branches. But as he addresses the ball, say casually, 'I don't want to put you off, old chap, but did you know that technically you've already lost the hole? You see you asked me to help you find your ball and I'm afraid that under Rule 42 it is forbidden to request an opponent to help you in any way. Penalty: loss of hole or two strokes.'

His fingers may now begin to twitch, so add hastily, 'But I don't think we need bother about it, need we? I mean it's not as if we were playing strict rules. In any case I've an idea the penalty may be disqualification from the match.'

The effect of all this will be to prepare the ground for any subsequent breaches of rule by yourself and will place the opponent in your debt (see previous chapter —'Emotion').

But frequently it is not possible to be present for an opponent's stroke.

The only clue to an opponent's progress then is muffled cries as he hacks down the rough a hundred yards the other side of the fairway.

Unfortunately the average Coarse Golfer cannot be

trusted to count his own strokes. This is not because he is a cheat. But he is subject to Law Eight of Coarse Golf which states :

'When counting his strokes a Coarse Golfer will ignore one in four.'

This is done quite unconsciously. A doctor friend with a knowledge of psychiatry assures me it is due to a Coarse Golfer's refusal to face up to the facts of life. Being unable to meet the fearful truth that he is not any good at the game, he unconsciously compensates by lying to himself (Coarse Golf Self-deception Syndrome).

Not that my medical friend is entirely reliable in these matters. For years he has refused to believe that any of his patients are actually ill. You can go to him groaning with pain and he'll just say, 'It's all in the mind, old boy. Stop worrying about your work. Anyway, pain is merely a symptom. It's the cause that needs treating.'

Then one Sunday morning he slipped in the mud while climbing up to the plateau hole and twisted his knee. I have never heard such screams of agony in my whole life.

We tried to comfort him by telling him it was all in the mind, and anyway pain was merely a symptom, but he wouldn't listen, shouting instructions for stretchers and for pain-killers and groaning, 'You don't understand how much it hurts.'

He is also inclined to be a little unreliable in adding up his own number of strokes. In fact Askew has not played with him since a furious argument which ended with Askew saying, 'You ought to see a psychiatrist.'

Self-deception is not confined to Coarse Golf. Most of us do it throughout our daily life, telling ourselves that our balding heads still have plenty of hair, that our bulging waists are as slim as ever, and that young women are smiling at us on trains.

But however common this failing, it is necessary to have a defence against an opponent's little human weakness.

Listen carefully, therefore, to the sounds made by him as these will give a clue to the real number of strokes.

Unfortunately, it is not possible to say there will be one stroke per howl, shout or curse. If that were so, there would be no problem.

But upon finding a ball in a bad lie a Coarse Golfer immediately utters an oath without making a stroke (the Primary Curse). He then sizes up the situation and in the guise of addressing the ball swishes his club carefully to remove all obstacles from around the ball. He then makes a stroke which sends earth in all directions and the ball nowhere, and utters the Secondary Curse.

This process is repeated all over again, perhaps several times, until either the ball is struck clear or, more likely, he becomes tired of the whole thing and moves the ball to a better lie or even throws it out of the rough, emerging with a bland expression and a shout of 'playing two'.

If case this should seem exaggerated, let me quote a genuine example.

When playing N. Batley in 1960, I saw him vanish into a deep bunker. Four little spurts of sand then shot high into the air, each one followed by an oath. Finally a hand came over the top of the bunker and threw the ball on to the green.

Batley then clambered out covered in sand and said, 'Playing three. This old eight iron is simply wonderful in bunkers.'

When I taxed him to tell the truth he replied, 'You can't take a joke, old man,' thus putting me in the defensive position.

A formula that will put an end to such embarrassing incidents and will give the true number of strokes taken by an opponent is as follows:

The number of shots taken by an opponent who is out of sight is equal to the square root of the sum of the number of curses heard plus the number of swishes.

Or,

$$\sqrt{Curse + swishes} = strokes$$

Thus, where A is the number of curses and B the number of swishes, then the number of strokes is:

$$\sqrt{A+B}$$

Example: When there are two unsuccessful strokes followed by one successful, then normally there will be three oaths and nine swishes. (There are no oaths and only one swish on the successful shot.)

Where the curses are three and the swishes nine we have:

$$\sqrt{3+9}$$

or the square root of twelve which is between three and four, this being the approximate number of strokes.

To make best use of the formula, strike first, using these three golden rules:

Do not reveal your score to the opponent.

Do not let him reveal his score to you.

Tell him what his score was before he can say anything.

As soon as he's within range shout, 'Rotten luck taking five strokes to get out of the wood, wasn't it, old man?' Ignore anything he has said previously to the contrary.

What follows is like the conversation between two second-hand-car dealers swindling each other, with bid followed by counter-bid and expressions of surprise and ruination all round, until eventually some sort of compromise on the number of strokes is arrived at.

But by striking first one can ensure that all the bargaining is based on the figure you choose, which by reason of the formula will be a fairly accurate one. And that is half the battle, as any car dealer, estate agent, horse-thief or crook will tell you.

During bargaining, try to anticipate an opponent's attack on your score. Pretend to hear nothing he has said and remark: 'You want to watch out for snakes in the wood.'

'Snakes?'

'Yes, I had to keep swishing at 'em with my five iron to scare them away. Probably sounded as if I was taking a shot each time.'

(Note: A useful alternative to snakes are voles, rats and any vermin, including children.)

Do not be depressed if, despite this, the opposition are three or four strokes up on arrival at the green. Remember a Coarse Golfer never concedes a hole, except when he wants to put in a good card, and he then concedes numerous holes, counting one more stroke than his opponent.

The glorious uncertainty of Coarse Golf, as against the machine-like monotony of the ordinary game, is one of its chief glories.

When I was playing W. Rudderham at Hanwell in 1961, Rudderham actually conceded a hole *on the tee* after sending five balls into the River Brent.

My own drive had, by some lapse on the part of the gods, crossed the river, and I played out the hole to see if I could beat my previous best score there (eight).

I crossed the bridge, took an eight iron and hit a ball straight into another loop of the river. I put down a second and hit it exactly where the first went. I swear it landed in the same patch of foam.

It was obviously a case for emergency procedures. I therefore adopted Coarse Golf Emergency Drill No. 1, turned at forty-five degrees to the pin, concentrated like hell, and aimed at a spot 100 yards to the left of the green. At the last moment I decided things were going too well so I tried to open up the clubface and encourage my natural slice. I never did find out what happened to the ball but this time the club landed in the river.

As I put down my fourth ball I was surprised to see my opponent seize his trolley and start running back to the tee, waving his club at the pair behind and shouting maniacally. For a moment I thought he must have been eating prunes again—they sometimes have that effect on him.

'Where are you going?' I cried in alarm.

'Back to the tee,' he shouted. 'I withdraw my concession of the hole.'

This so shattered me that I took a modest fourteen and we halved.

I don't think a true Coarse Golfer would ever refuse to let an opponent withdraw his concession of the hole, even though I have known a man who did it on the green, marching solemnly back 550 yards to the tee and then hacking his way back again, fifty yards at a time.

But I draw the line at a habit of Askew's, who, if he loses a ball on the third, and then finds it while playing the tenth, wants to go back and play the third all over again.

As Coarse Golfers frequently play out of turn, one player may well arrive on the green ahead of the others. If you are the lucky one, use the opportunity to good advantage, leaning nonchalantly on a club, tapping the foot and looking at the watch.

My Uncle Walter has a special watch for this, an

old-fashioned turnip which he pulls out ostentatiously whenever he wishes to suggest to his opponent that he is lagging.

Even if there is no bargaining to be done over the score conceal your number of strokes from the opponent. Coarse Golfers always seek reassurance as to the state of the game before they putt. Do not give this reassurance. Pretend not to hear the question, walk away to your trolley, or if pressed be vague about the whole business.

'How many strokes? You are curious, aren't you, Fred? Well, there was my drive . . . that was one . . . or did I have another off the tee? . . . no, that was at the fourth . . . well, that makes one then . . . and then I took out a five iron . . . or was it a six? . . . no, I remember, it must have been a five . . .'

If this sort of gibberish is continued long enough the opponent may well be reduced to a neurotic frenzy which will wreck his putt.

Always give an opponent perfectly genuine information about the state of the green. Tell him quite honestly what you think it's doing and how the nap is lying.

He won't believe a word. I have only to tell Askew the green is running fast and he promptly belts the ball ten feet beyond the pin, muttering 'Damn liar' to himself all the time.

Under no circumstances do anything that would distract an opponent while putting. Such a thing would be despicable. Make it perfectly plain that you are *not* going to distract him.

Tend That Pin!

IT'S NO **USE**, MIKE, ALL MY OPPONENTS PUTT **BETTER** THAN I DO!

WELL, DON'T JUST STAND THERE... WHAT ARE YOU **DOING** ABOUT IT?

COUGH! COUGH! COUGH! COUGH!

I AM **DISGUSTED** WITH YOU, ALF! THAT IS JUST **CRUDE!** AND BESIDES IT DOESN'T **WORK!** YOU SHOULD ALWAYS **TEND THE PIN!** NOW, WATCH ME!

TRY TO GET A PUTT DOWN **NOW!**

YOU SEE! NO ONE CAN FACE THIS APPARITION! BUT NO ONE CAN ACCUSE YOU OF CHEATING! YOU ARE MERELY **TRYING** TO KEEP STILL!

Jack o' the Green

I usually say something like, 'Look, old chap, this is a very important putt for you so for heaven's sake tell me if I am distracting you in any way. I do know that sometimes even the sound of breathing puts some people off but don't worry, I shall be holding my breath.'

I then pad slowly across his line of vision and tiptoe round behind him, a cigarette in my mouth and holding a box of matches and a match, which I do not strike.

'Don't worry,' I call out, 'I shall *not* strike the match.'

If asked to tend the pin, emphasise again that you are not going to distract anybody. Freeze rigid as soon as the opponent starts his preliminaries, if possible in some fantastic position, perhaps on one leg with an arm held vertically.

At the same time I always stare maniacally at my opponent's left knee. He becomes uneasily aware of this and may interrupt his address to ask me to relax. In this case I take up another pose even more contorted than the first.

No sound must be permitted while a putt is being taken, but if it should be too strong, an occasional cry of 'Fore!' is permissible.

So much for an opponent's putting. What about your own?

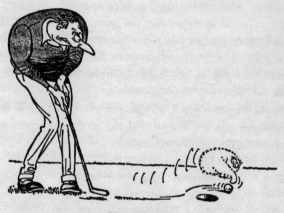

The Zobbergeist

Remember a putt is not made with a club and ball. It is made with the mind. Everyone knows perfectly well whether a putt will go down before the stroke is made. And if it is going down then it doesn't matter whether you stand on your head and whistle *God Save the Queen* as you putt, it will still go in.

Bad putting is usually caused by evil spirits, the two most common being Jack o' the Green and the Zobbergeist.

Jack o' the Green is about six inches long and wears a little pointed hat. I know because I've seen him. He stands on the green and pulls at the head of the putter so it won't go back straight. Sometimes he even perches on the toe of the club as you try to hit the ball.

The Zobbergeist is almost invisible and specialises in hovering over the ball and turning it aside when by all rights it ought to slap down the middle of the hole. He is difficult to see but you sometimes just catch a glimpse of a sort of lump fluttering over the ball as it swings round the edge of the hole. At times he emits a tiny hum.

According to legend, any player who sees Jack o' the Green will lose the round. An old professional in Sussex told me the traditional rhyme:

> When Jack o' the Green be see
> Beaten five and four you be.
> But if the Zobbergeist you do hear
> Then stuff your putter in your ear.

Evil spirits, however, only operate when the player's mind is obsessed with golf. They *know*. The most effective way of counteracting them is to concentrate on something as far removed from golf as possible. Concentration on the stroke, as recommended by all leading authorities, is worse than useless. It offends the spirits.

I find it helps to imagine that the ball is resting on the stomach of a naked woman. While those who have played with me will say that this accounts for a lot, I still maintain that it is enough to relax the tension.

My Uncle Walter always pretends that my aunt is standing by the hole and if he gets the ball into it, a mine will explode and blow her up.

Keen students will doubtless be able to think up their own putting fantasies. It is all yet another example of how the imaginary is more important than the reality in Coarse Golf.

8

Some Classic Coarse Strokes

'They have slain the Earl of Murray
And laid him on the green.'

OLD BALLAD

One of the glories of Coarse Golf is its variety of strokes.
There are as many different types as in cricket. In fact,
some of them are derived from cricket rather than
golf, while others owe much to the inspiration of the
hockey field. At least one of my own favourite strokes
is the result of playing softball against an American
unit during the war.

This is yet another example of the greater interest
aroused by the Coarse Game as opposed to ordinary
golf, where there is basically only one swing, with minor
adjustments according to the club and the situation.

The variety of strokes in Coarse Golf is not deliberate. As far as a Coarse Golfer's mind is concerned he is
playing the same stroke every time—a smooth, con-
trolled, compact swing which is effortlessly going to send
the ball to within inches of the target.

The most frequently employed Coarse Golf stroke is
the *Knurdle*.

This occurs when a player feels he can *just* make the green from 210 yards if he 'gives it a good belt with a three iron'.

Preliminary signs that a *Knurdle* is about to be made are a swelling of the veins of neck and face, heavy panting and frequent, savage looks towards the green while addressing the ball. Often a continual low muttering noise is uttered, together with religious vows, such as 'By God, I'm going to ...'

The patient clutches the club as if his life depends on it and takes a backswing which in extreme cases is actually more than 360 degrees, the clubhead finishing by the ankle.

Then, with a wild howl, he aims a desperate lunge at the ball, but even before he has hit it he has lifted his head and is peering hopefully towards the green.

There has never yet been a recorded instance of a *Knurdle* connecting fair and square with the ball, which would undoubtedly burst if this did happen. Sometimes the ball is driven into the ground, although more often than not the patient misses altogether or strikes the earth a foot behind the ball.

On hard ground he will then dance around in agony and hurl away the club, so stand well clear of a *Knurdler*.

The *Knurdle* is equally applicable to a wood or iron shot, the only criterion being that the target, be it green or fairway, must just be within reach of a well-struck ball.

The inevitable failure of the stroke is first followed

by exclamations of sheer disbelief as the patient stares at the ball, which has not moved. This is then followed by a long statement of what went wrong.

Inevitably, the patient blames it all on some trifling fault such as breaking the wrists too soon or standing too near the ball. He will not accept the suggestion that he tried to hit it too hard.

Under no circumstances disagree or try to argue with a *Knurdler,* as he may become violent and abusive. Enter into the spirit of the thing and blame the position of his right hip, left elbow, etc. Suggest his little finger is curled too far round the club.

Near the greens, another frequently seen stroke is the *Jobble.*

It usually happens when a player is making a deliberate and determined effort to relax consciously and for this reason often follows a *Knurdle,* as a reaction from the violence of that stroke. It also frequently occurs after a patient has been over-hitting his chips.

The club involved is generally a nine, eight or seven. The patient walks up to the ball with exaggerated ease, swinging his club jauntily and hurls away his cigarette with nonchalance. He glances at the hole, notes the position of the bunkers, and then addresses the ball with a strange swaying motion, like a reptile listening to a snake-charmer's pipe.

The clubhead is twitched frequently without purpose after which the player changes the position of his feet. Just when the watchers have given up all hope that he will ever hit the ball he suddenly sways backwards like a sapling in the wind, looks up at the sky, and using only the wrists flicks the club over the top of the ball, or else scrapes it two or three feet along the ground.

Normally, the ball will at once enter the nearest bunker.

Upon making the stroke the patient stares fixedly at a spot midway between his feet, where the ball may well still be, and calls upon heaven and various other higher authorities to witness that he did everything the pro/instruction book/coaching film/pamphlet, etc., told him.

He will then spend ten minutes repeating the stroke without the ball and calling upon the other players to witness that he did it right, he did everything they said, so they were all wrong and he was right. In extreme cases he may have to be dragged away before the game can continue.

From this stroke is derived the adjective '*jobbly*', denoting a condition in which the wrists apparently turn to jelly and all control is lost over the club. For example, 'I hit a lovely wood but went all *jobbly* near the green.'

A player suffering from a *Jobble* will find it a distressing and persistent condition, made worse by the fact that he really is trying to do what everyone says, and relax. Things are worse if other people sympathise. Always shower sympathy on an opponent who *jobbles*.

Only last year a *Jobble* cost me five pounds. Playing

against S. Clemens at Coombe Wood, I was four feet short of the green with a three iron at a short hole. When Clemens put his tee shot into a cross-bunker I fell about laughing so much that with his face suffused with anger he bet me five pounds his next shot would land nearer the pin than mine.

Clemens then walked into the bunker, took a casual glance towards the green and without addressing the ball hit it 60 yards to within six feet of the pin. I spent five minutes trying to relax on my chip, caught a fearful attack of the *jobbles* and succeeded in moving the ball four feet, losing five pounds and the match.

From this it will be realised that the *Jobble* is the shot of a man with something on his mind (in my case, five pounds). Hence married men are particularly liable to *Jobble*. It is the gay bachelor who *Knurdles*.

A stroke which can be produced on either the tee or the green is *Rigor Mortis*. On the tee, it is the result of loss of confidence in the wooden clubs.

Determined to do everything as the books says, the patient slowly lifts the club back with the arms completely rigid, his eyes bulging with the effort of keeping them fixed on the ball. There is a moment's terrible pause at the top of the backswing, and then, still keeping his arms stiff, the patient slowly lowers the club-head on to the ball, rather as if he was afraid it would explode.

On the green, the patient finds he is suddenly unable to control his limbs. The result is usually that extraordinary stroke, a hooked putt. Until a player has seen a well-hooked putt, his golf experience is incomplete.

Another interesting little stroke is the *Blütt und Thunderworst*. This term was invented by Askew to describe an all-out assault on a ball in the rough, in a bad lie or a bunker. It would be impossible in ordinary golf, for reasons which will appear obvious, and is thus confined to the Coarse Game.

In a *Blütt und Thunderworst* the club is whirled round and round in a continuous arc without ceasing, fanning the air just above the ball. Askew claims that provided the movement is absolutely unbroken this counts as only one stroke, since the club never comes to rest.

Skilled operators of the *B.u.T.* gradually lower the clubhead as it passes over the top of the ball until some sort of contact is made.

The main disadvantage of this stroke is the danger of breaking the wrists if the clubhead should suddenly strike an obstruction such as a stone.

A derivation of the *B.u.T.* is the *Gezundheit!* This is normally employed by a player who is feeling good. He strolls up to the ball, pulls out a club, weighs it in his hand for a moment and then, with a merry cry, strikes at the ball which remains unimpressed by the whole affair.

As with most Coarse strokes the patient is quite unable to grasp why he failed. The most irritating thing that an opponent can say, is to call out cheerfully '*Gezundheit!*' immediately after the shot.

I sometimes find it effective to say, 'And for my next

trick . . .', 'Thank you, Mr. Nureyev', or 'Don't ring us, we'll ring you'.

A stroke always performed accidentally is the *Oozeleum*. I am indebted to a friend, Mr. Basil Harben, for the invention of this stroke while playing with his managing director.

Basil was partnering his boss in a foursome. Not only was he anxious to make a good impression but he was under the handicap of having to justify his own exaggeration, having unwisely boasted of his prowess to the managing director before he knew there was any danger of having to prove it.

At the first hole Basil's boss drove 230 yards straight down the middle. Basil, with his iron shot, immediately hit the ball with immense force into a nearby bunker, where it buried itself in the sand.

With a wonderful recovery shot, the managing director retrieved the situation and left the ball in the middle of the fairway about 150 yards from the green.

'And don't make a mess of it this time,' he snarled as Basil addressed the ball.

Basil delayed striking the ball for as long as he could, even interrupting his address to tie his shoelace, but eventually he was forced to make the fatal move. Actually, it was one of his better shots, since it did at least have distance, and if playing me he would have danced around with glee.

Unfortunately, the ball was possessed of a fearsome hook, and it vanished into a small wood of fir trees to the back and left of the green.

They watched it vanish in silence and the managing director turned to Basil and said simply : 'Clot.'

Basil did not reply. He stood staring in the direction of the green for a moment and then, with his jaw agape, feebly gestured towards the pin.

His employer turned in time to see their ball rebound from the woods, roll gently up to the stick, hit it, and settle down six inches from the hole.

At this point Basil could undoubtedly have been made a director had he played his cards right, but he spoiled everything by saying, 'It's my natural draw, sir. Most big hitters have it.'

I mention the story to show that in Coarse Golf a ball is never dead until it's stopped moving and that an *Oozeleum* is always 'on' notwithstanding the fact that the ball may actually have passed the green.

Incidentally, an *Oozeleum* is sometimes known among the cognoscenti as an *Askew*. Strictly an *Askew* is any shot which returns to the fairway or green through means of an outside agency such as hitting a trolley, shed or tree, and is named after my friend Askew because of his uncanny predilection for this sort of thing.

In fact, ever since driving from the first and holing out on the eighteenth via the assistant professional, Askew claims to have done the course in one and boasts that his handicap is plus 67.

Because of my Uncle Walter's fondness for the same stroke Coarse Golfers will often use the expression, 'I gave him an Askew for his Walter', meaning, of course, that he gave him a Roland for his Oliver.

The strokes so far described are all largely accidental, but there are some strokes peculiar to Coarse Golf which are made deliberately.

First I shall describe the *Scrape*. This is a deliberate topping of the ball and is used chiefly for getting out of bunkers, especially in wet weather when the sand is firm.

A well-topped ball will then skim over the surface of the sand and into safety. Using this stroke I have got out of a bunker in as few as three strokes. It may also be used when a low trajectory is needed, such as when playing out from underneath a bush.

To make a *Scrape*, address the ball as for a normal bunker shot, aiming to strike the sand about two inches behind the ball, and then fix the eyes on some object on the skyline, such as a tree. Keeping the eyes rigidly focused on the skyline, play the shot as for a normal stroke. Do not look down under any circumstances.

The *Sweep* is another useful shot when in trouble and is played when there is a steep uphill lie, or the ball is on the banks of a stream. Kneel down on the downhill side of the ball, until the ball is level with the shoulders, and then swing the club horizontally as if wielding a baseball bat. Strike the ball with the heel of the club. Try not to fall into the stream after the stroke.

The *Squeeze* is one of the most difficult shots in the Coarse Golfer's armoury but one of the most rewarding. It is used when a ball cannot be played in the normal way because it is lying close to a tree or similar obstruction which inhibits the backswing.

The secret is to take up a strance two feet in front of the ball, so that during the address the clubhead is vertically over the ball. Then raise the clubhead to shoulder height and bring it down on the back of the ball with a smart vertical action, at the same time crying 'Whoops-a-daisy'.

The ball (with luck) will then shoot into the air at an angle of forty-five degrees. Be careful it doesn't hit you in the face. I have not spoken to an old friend since, while I was trying this shot, the ball struck me on the jaw and as I was writhing on the ground he claimed two strokes penalty.

Finally we come to the *Walter Lindrum,* named after the great snooker player. This is one of the most

The 'Walter Lindrum' stroke

simple yet effective shots in the Coarse Game and is used most frequently for getting out from underneath bushes. Using this stroke, many players have got out of trouble in as few as four shots.

The technique is extraordinarily simple. The player merely lies down behind the ball and plays it with the end of the shaft of his club, as if it were a billiard or snooker ball (hence the name).

If an opponent says this is illegal, ask him to name the rule which says the ball must be struck with the head of the club. I can't find it.

It is difficult to get much distance with a *Lindrum*, but the ball can usually be sent far enough to clear the bush.

The stroke can also be used in a bad lie within a foot or so of the fairway, but I do not recommend it on the putting green unless you are out of sight of the clubhouse, as stuffy club officials seem to object to players crawling all over the greens.

9

Hazards

'He putteth down one, and setteth up another.'
PSALM 75, VERSE 8

In order to be as successful as possible within his limited
capabilities it is essential for a Coarse Golfer to have a
thorough understanding of the hazards to be encountered on a course, artificial, natural, human and super-
natural.

Among those that must loom large are water
hazards.

I think it was Arnold Palmer who in an article in a
golf magazine was asked to describe what he thought
would be a perfect course.

It was quite obvious that his ideas of the game and
mine differed widely and his scheme for a perfect hole
was something six hundred yards long, shaped like an
elephant's trunk, and with a fairway three feet wide
surrounded by swamps. Come to think of it, I'm not
sure he even had a fairway at all.

His favourite hole, however, was the water-hole.
Mr. Palmer's plan for this was a tiny island, entirely

surrounded by a great lake and accessible only by means of a small footbridge. The idea, as he remarked, was to penalise the man who did not go for the hole.

While my immediate reaction was one of pity for Mr. Palmer (I mean, surely he can't really get any fun out of the game) he is quite right about the effect of water on a golfer.

Golf balls are attracted to water as unerringly as the eye of a middle-aged man to a female bosom. If a patch of water is placed twenty yards in front of a Coarse Golfer he will not merely hit his first shot into it, but the second and third as well.

Desperately mesmerised he will continue to send ball after ball to a watery grave, unless physically restrained, and even then I have known men who had had to be dragged away by force, shouting, 'Give me just one more chance, I know I can get over this time.'

My Uncle Walter once put five balls in succession into the River Brent, followed by his clubs and then himself. He was dragged out by a greenkeeper, calling, 'Let me drown, why did you have to save me?'

Personally I don't see why a player should not capitalise on the water-neurosis, and I always encourage my opponent to have another go.

The simplest way of doing this is to step forward, lay a brotherly hand on the sleeve and say earnestly, 'Look, old man, why not take an iron and chip up to the edge?'

The opponent, who will still be rolling his eyes wildly in the direction of the hazard, will reject the advice with an impatient twitch, and select another ball from his dwindling supply, muttering, 'This time I'm going to get it over.'

From then on it is merely necessary to feed the flames with an occasional 'Don't be a fool, old boy, you'll never do it', etc., etc.

One hesitates on such dangerous ground to give any advice on how to overcome a water hazard although I can tell how to make certain of landing in it—play a new ball. Provided one can induce the dreaded water-neurosis into an opponent, it is hardly necessary to play the hazard.

Some years ago I played against a man who topped his drive so badly that it skipped over the surface of a lake in a series of jumps and landed safely the other side. But I don't think he made a habit of this.

One method of coping is to aim deliberately to land smack in the middle of the water. The same dodge can be used when a tree blocks the path to the green. Aim at the tree.

This is based on the theory that a Coarse Golfer will never hit what he is aiming at. But such is the perversity of Fate that frequently he does hit it. I still have the scar on my face as a souvenir of the time when I aimed carefully at a tiny pine tree twelve feet away and hit it dead centre.

So be prepared for disappointment and play your oldest ball.

One of the joys of Coarse Golf is the interesting people encountered around water hazards, under bridges and so forth. There is a course in Kent where

Tree Tactics

one of the greenkeeper's sons stands in the middle of a stream dressed in rubber waders, pocketing balls as they land.

He is a strange, silent youth, saying nothing, and deaf to all insults, threats and appeals for the return of the ball, even when money is offered. His stamina must be considerable, for he never leaves his post until the course is clear when he retires with his haul to his father, who sells them to the pro. Eventually they filter back to the members at 2*s*. 6*d*. a time via the pro's shop.

The strangest experience I ever had at a water hazard was in the West Country.

Playing on a clifftop course, I was faced with the choice of hitting to the green 170 yards across a small cove, at the bottom of which raged the Atlantic Ocean, or chipping back to the fairway and wasting a stroke.

As I was trying to make up my mind a man's face appeared over the edge of the cliff. He was old and bearded and covered in seagull droppings, a sort of Ben Gunn dressed in a blue sweater.

'Have a go, zur,' shouted the apparition. 'You could make that green easily with a three iron. You mark my words. Ar.'

With that he sank back and his face disappeared behind the cliff. All was silent except for the cries of gulls and the roar of the surf.

At first I thought I had been visited by some shade, perhaps the ghost of James Braid, who'd been watch-

'Have a go, zur,' shouted the apparition

ing my progress for years and had at last decided to step in and take a hand himself. Finally I decided I must have imagined the whole affair. But taking the visitation's advice I selected a three iron and swung mightily in a great *Knurdle*.

The ball trickled twenty yards and disappeared over the cliff. I ran to the edge and peered down. The old man was at the bottom, fifty feet below, putting my ball into a big sack.

'Bad luck, zur,' he shouted above the wind. 'Why don't 'ee have another go with a four wood?' And with that he carried his sack of balls into a cave.

They told me at the clubhouse that he rowed to the cove every day in the summer and spent his time encouraging strangers to have a go at the green. He was also suspected of hanging out lights to wreck ships.

Strangely enough, although a Coarse Golfer regards water of any sort as a terrible hazard, he is liable to treat bunkers with contempt. My own view is that if the ball is in a bunker at least you know where it is, which is more than can be said of a great many shots, and at least it's reasonably near the fairway. After years of trying to play from open sewers, ditches, drains and so on a bunker presents few problems.

The club must not be grounded in a bunker but I see no reason why one should not pace to and fro across the sand, just behind the ball, examining the lie and so forth. Stones may be removed, and if there should be a large stone just behind the ball, or even the suspicion of a stone, so much the better.

A bigger hazard than bunkers are greenkeepers.

One day I shall start a fund to provide green-keepers with reliable and silent engines to their mowers. It is a law of Coarse Golf that upon the golfer taking the most vital putt of the game, a greenkeeper will appear with a motor mower.

He may then continue to mow without any reference to players, especially if he thinks they are visitors or society members.

More likely he will wheel the mower up to within three feet of the putter, and throttle back the motor. As this is always abominably looked after, with plugs like a sweep's brush, the player has to make his stroke with a sort of 'Chug-chug-chug-chug-BOOM-chug-chug-chug-chug-chug-PSSSST-chug-chug-chug-WURP . . .' going on behind him.

It would not be so bad if the odd explosion came in a regular sequence but it is impossible to anticipate it, except to say that it usually occurs when one is irretrievably committed to the putt.

When a player has missed his putt the greenkeeper will stare at him with a look of bovine insolence, which has been known to drive golfers to physical violence, and rev up the engine violently.

Because a Coarse Golfer is so often playing on public course, common land and so forth, courting couples can be a serious nuisance. I don't know whether it's simply *me*, but I always seem to be stumbling over them all over every golf course. I've only got to start a round for it to act as a signal for every young lover in the shire to woo his lass, frequently in the rough near the fourteenth.

The only consolation is that this is obviously as old as the game itself. Witness the mediaeval Scottish ballad *Clerk Saunders,* which contains the telling lines :

> Clerk Saunders and May Margaret
> Walked o'er yon gravelled green
> And sad and heavy was the love
> I wot, it fell these two between.

True, I haven't actually come across anyone consummating an affair on the green, whether gravelled or otherwise, but I've come across some pretty odd goings-on on other parts of the course. I've no doubt the writer was sick and tired of reaching the green with a nice swipe from his cleek only to find Clerk Saunders and May Margaret writhing all over it.

These days, poor old Askew's sexual balance is so disturbed that the mere sight of someone holding a girl's hand fills him with an uncontrollable lust, so that he is quite incapable of playing the simplest stroke.

'By golly,' he mutters, as with trembling hands he attempts to address the ball, 'did you see that dark-haired piece with that young yob behind the green?' All virile young men are 'yobs' to Askew.

I tend to feed his lust for my own purposes by idly quoting from the Song of Solomon ('Thy navel is like a goblet and thy breasts are . . .' etc. etc.) or else expounding on some point of the woman's anatomy that he might have missed.

This wheeze is worth a stroke or two with the right opponent, but should not be used if one is equally vulnerable to amorous propensities yourself, or else the round will degenerate into bawdy reminiscences.

Women golfers have changed from the days when tweed-skirted Amazons looking like Mother Courage prowled the course with cigarettes in holders, and they can prove a serious distraction, especially if wearing tight trousers.

If an opponent should comment on their beauty, it is worth pointing out that it is a sign of old age when women golfers look desirable. Emphasise that when he was younger they didn't look attractive and the female form cannot have changed *that* much, so he must be getting old.

As regards the courting couples, unless they are actually on the green or in a bunker it is useless to suggest that they move. For one thing they always have a pathetic ignorance about golf, being under the impression that the ball will go where you hit it, and that if you aim to avoid them then they are safe.

The biggest difficulty lies in convincing them, if the ball should strike them, that it was an accident on your part and not sheer jealousy.

SUDDEN APPEARANCE OF ELDERLY IDIOT

This is another hazard peculiar to Coarse Golf and one which again emphasises how easy life is for the first-class player, spending his life on courses which are strictly private.

Where the public have any means of access at all, such as a footpath across the course, it is a law of Coarse Golf that during a vital stroke an old fool will suddenly appear and stand behind the player wheezing.

Wimbledon Common in particular abounds in them. They have a knack of turning up just as one is putting to save the match.

There's not much that can be done about it. It is useless to wait for them to move on because they consider they are doing a favour hanging around three feet behind you and making little burbling noises through their pipes. Besides, they're interested. They like to stroll over the course every morning and watch the agonies of the players.

Upon the putt being missed, they then say, 'Ah, I could see you was going to miss that one, young-feller-me-lad', or some similar pleasantry calculated to drive a normal person insane. One of the symptoms of these people is that all golfers under 60 are young-feller-me-lads.

The only advice I can give is this: since it is impossible to make them go away before you play, at least make sure they remain for the opponent's stroke. Detain them in harmless gossip and then caution them to silence and stillness, ignoring any muttered remarks from the green like, 'Why don't you tell the old fool to —— off', etc., etc.

It was at Wimbledon, by the way, that I had the

unusual experience of being turned off the course by a man on horseback.

If anyone had forecast this would happen to me I would have declared him mad, but there we were playing the first (Elcho as the London Scottish call it, or Muck-up as I know it), when a chap galloped up on a bay mare rather as if he had just heard some particularly good news in Aix and wanted to get it to Ghent as quickly as possible.

'You must stop playing,' he called, reining in Black Bess, or whatever she was called. 'I am a Common Conservator.'

'I'm Liberal myself,' I replied, 'but I respect all views.'

'You'll have to leave the course. It is forbidden to play here unless you are wearing a red coat.'

Ha, ha, jolly funny,' I replied, humouring him. 'Now if you'll kindly move your horse I'll just pitch the ball up to the green.'

It took him half an hour to convince us that he was not insane, and that it *is* illegal to play golf on Wimbledon Common without a red coat.

Because the course is on common land the public have priority and golfers must be plainly marked, like the lepers of old. It is also illegal to shout 'Fore'. You just have to wait for people to move.

Palmer, old chap, you haven't seen anything.

The list of hazards on courses open to the public are endless—horses on the fairway, people picnicking on the greens, dogs fouling the tees, cross-country runners popping up as you drive.

No wonder some of us are so bad. I don't think even Gary Player could drive successfully with a horse fertilising the tee as he addressed the ball.

ARMED MEN PATROLLING COURSE

I am indebted to an old friend, Mr. Richard Field, of Northampton, for a description of the most unusual hazard I have ever heard of.

While playing at a course in Arizona, he noticed that players who hit balls into a shallow water hazard never bothered to collect them.

Being a hard-up Englishman he therefore paddled in and began to fill his bag when he was arrested by an armed sheriff patrolling the course with two six-guns and a ten-gallon hat.

Perhaps the fact that Richard greeted him by saying, 'Where did you come from? A cornflake packet?' may have had something to do with it.

The sheriff could not believe that anyone would want to waste time salvaging a lost ball and decided that the English Coarse Golfers must have been connected with something illegal, such as fishing with dynamite.

Richard explained that Englishmen always salvage any balls they can, as so many are lost due to the fog which permanently envelops the country, and he was released with a warning.

10

Behaviour

'Bear-like, I must fight the course . . .'

MACBETH

The general rule of etiquette in Coarse Golf seems to
be that solo players have right of way over all matches.
It is not normally necessary for them to ask permission
to play through—they simply pound on round the
course, frequently arriving on the green at the same
time as the players in front.

If a rule can be formulated, it is that the match
which reaches the green first shall take precedence. This
makes for an interesting situation when two different
matches are both chipping on to the green from
bunkers on opposite sides, so that everyone is criss-
crossing the green as if in a ghastly square dance.

A five-ball has priority over everything else.

A five-ball usually consists of five burly men in over-
alls and cycle clips, with one set of clubs between them.
They are not only the slowest players on the course
but also the most resentful of being overtaken.
Attempts to remonstrate will be met with abuse and

threats of violence ('What's the hurry, mate? You don't own the bloomin' golf pitch, you know').

Askew and I once suffered the torture of having to play behind a *seven-ball*, with only one set of clubs between the lot of them. They were spread all over the countryside like a platoon on manœuvres, and dashing about borrowing clubs from each other. Sometimes they even threw them across the fairway.

After the first hole, which took them twenty-five minutes, we tried to go through but they didn't understand the rules and thought we were queue-jumping. The more we tried to go through the faster they played, hitting the ball fifty yards and then running after it and hitting it again in an effort to keep ahead.

The result was that Askew and I became inextricably mixed up with the lot of them and the seven-ball became a *nine-ball* from which we couldn't escape, because one of them borrowed Askew's six iron and took it into the bushes.

The first two holes took nearly an hour, after which we made a terrific effort and got a little ahead. We were just about to drive from the fourth when all seven of them filed out of a spinney and on to the tee. Apparently six players had conceded the previous hole and they'd caught us up.

Askew took one look at them and whispered, 'We've got to get away from this lot. Whatever you do, make sure your drive is a good one.'

With which, he sent his drive straight into a quarry ten yards in front of the tee. I was determined not to follow him, and by George I didn't. I didn't even reach the edge of the quarry. However, my second shot did, and rolled down beside Askew's.

We were miserably scrambling down the sides when there came the sound of a stroke and a ball flashed overhead, to the accompaniment of a loud cheer from the tee.

It was the ultimate disgrace. We had been over-taken by a seven-ball.

We hid in the quarry until they had gone and then went back to the clubhouse, only to find we couldn't even go home because their cars were blocking ours.

Women, under the mistaken impression that they play worse than men, will often wave male golfers through simply on the grounds of their sex. Do not take advantage of their courtesy.

The last time I did this I rewarded the girls who had so kindly given way by striking one of them on the knee with my drive as they waited on the ladies' tee. When I last saw her she was being carried into a car.

On Wednesday afternoons, or whenever early clos-ing day may be, be prepared to find undertakers' mutes or trios of bereaved persons wandering all over the course, playing each stroke as if it was their last and then holding a committee meeting on the result.

There people are deaf to the ordinary courtesies of golf and even to pointed hints like driving over their heads (in which case they are quite likely to throw away your ball).

The only solution seems to be not to play golf on Wednesday afternoon.

LANGUAGE

The interesting thing about a Coarse Golfer's language is that to listen to him one would think that his bad shots came as a surprise.

Still, the results of bottling up a desire to swear can be dangerous, and it is far better to let fly.

A priest with whom I used to play always asked me, when things were too much to bear, to say it for him. I did this little service effectively and a great beam of content would spread over his features.

Askew's favourite remark is unfortunately Anglo-Saxon, but when women are near he tries to remove offence by adding the words, 'As D. H. Lawrence so adequately describes it', after each outburst.

Blasphemy should never be used. We all have deep-rooted guilt feelings as a result of early religious train-ing and any emotional relief will be more than offset by a nagging fear for the rest of the round that some terrible punishment will follow.

This underlying fear is responsible for wrecking many players' games without their knowing it, especially if there are thunderstorms about.

I well remember my Uncle Walter, who had been brought up most strictly in a lay preacher's family, hit-ting a near-perfect drive which struck a stone on the fairway and bounded off at right angles into a ditch.

Uncle Walter stood for a moment and then declared

firmly, 'There is no God, my boy, or He would not allow things like that to happen to His children.'

A few minutes later, after his game had become even worse and cumulus clouds were building up in the south, he came over to me and looking at the sky said loudly, 'Actually, I didn't mean that about there being no God. I did not mean it. Obviously there is a God.'

At the tenth there was quite definitely lightning about and I was recalling how some golfer had been electrocuted. By the thirteenth there was terrible thunder and Uncle Walter had started to peer over his shoulder as if he expected to find something perched there, muttering all the time, 'The fool hath said in his heart there is no God—Psalm 53.'

Not surprisingly he lost seven and five but refused to give me the ten shillings we normally have on the game, saying, 'Betting and swearing will get you nowhere, my boy.'

From this it will be seen that every Coarse Golfer must work out his own answer to the problem of swearing.

Personally, I always bellow at the top of my voice, 'Fornicazione'. It is a good word, and if anyone should complain I say it is an old Italian oath meaning, 'May my sister turn into a three-legged pig.'

GAMBLING

The time will eventually come when a Coarse Golfer is expected to back his skill with money.

He is generally at a great disadvantage in this, because although his real handicap would be thirty-nine if they went that far, the absurd rules of golf only allow him twenty-four, so that if he's playing anyone with a handicap of 24 or under he's going to lose hands down.

People with handicaps take advantage of this so a Coarse Golfer is perfectly entitled to demand odds, pointing out that his real handicap is 39, and if he can't have the correct number of strokes then he will have odds of three-to-one.

Most handicap golfers won't see the logic of this and think it is a joke. In that case be firm, and if the bet is five shillings hand over only one and eightpence at the end of the game. But be prepared to find that nobody will play with you again.

A more subtle way of evening-up things is to agree to the bet on level terms, but add little side bets during the game, e.g. betting your opponent a shilling he won't make the green. These side bets should always be negative, in other words based on your opponent's failing to do something. Never base them on a challenge to your own skill.

Usually an opponent will accept. Human nature cannot resist a challenge. In this way a Coarse Golfer may pick up three shillings during a round to compensate for the loss of five on the game.

Never have anything to do with people who specialise in complicated gambling schemes, such as:

'We usually have a rather odd sort of flutter, old chap. When a hole's finished you take the square root of the difference between the lowest number of strokes and the highest, and the loser pays twopence for every stroke. Then at the next hole you do the same, only this time the loser pays fourpence for every stroke, unless he wins the hole, in which case you go back to all square, and then if someone else wins the next hole *he* pays *you* twopence . . .'

Dazed by the explanation, which is invariably spoken at immense speed, the Coarse Golfer nods dumbly, and after two holes gives up any attempt to understand the economics of it, which, however, his opponent appears to comprehend perfectly, jotting down the details on a little pad which he never shows to anyone.

After the last putt on the eighteenth, the master gambler then turns round and says, 'Bad luck, old chap. I'm afraid you owe me three pounds, ten shillings and eightpence, counting that last putt you missed. Now if that had gone down it would have been only two pounds five and six.'

Any attempt to ask for a breakdown of this sum is met with a mass of figures, rather like a company chairman covering up a loss at the annual meeting. The Coarse Golfer gives up in despair and somehow finds himself paying for the round and the drinks as well.

It is as well to state plainly that golfers of this type are little better than professional cheats so a Coarse Golfer is perfectly entitled to argue the toss again and again, if he has the stamina, until the gambler gives up and takes it out on someone else.

Askew has a way of dealing with the situation which I do not recommend. He cheerfully accepts any system of betting, and even insists on doubling the stakes ('Not worth playing under a fiver, old chap'). Then when the round is finished and lost he bursts into roars of laughter and says, 'I thought you were joking. I never play for money.'

This way out can only be adopted if you do not object to going through life without friends.

THE CLUB

The old days, when all one needed to join a golf club was the signature of two members and an ability to pay the subscription, have gone. The first question asked of a prospective member is no longer, 'What car do you drive?' It is the dreaded, 'What is your handicap?'

However, the time may well come when a Coarse Golfer wishes to join a club. The difficulty is that these days no club will admit a new member without a handicap. But it is impossible to have a handicap unless you belong to a club. Impasse.

Fortunately, I can reveal a very simple way out of the dilemma, practised by myself on a number of occasions. All one has to do is to invent a mysterious and quite fictitious golfing society and award yourself 23. Twenty-four would be suspicious. It might be a nominal 24, but 23 presumably means one can play to that figure.

We are all snobs at heart and the best fictitious

society to invent is one connected with a profession (your own if possible, if not, someone else's).

'I've been a member of the Auctioneers' Golfing Society for years . . . we call them the Bidders, you know. Bongo Warrington's a great man there—former captain of Cambridge.'

A few phrases like that, and the figure '23' firmly written in the handicap space on your application form, will be good enough for most clubs.

But a word of warning. For five years I have belonged to a genuine golfing society with the unusual name of the Warreners, who in a moment of madness awarded me the low handicap of 22 (the chairman of the handicap committee owed me some money).

When I applied to join the London Scottish club I wrote boldly that my previous society was the Warreners and my handicap was 22.

Later the secretary came to me waving the form.

'These Warreners,' he said. 'Is it some kind of joke? I mean, no society has a name like that, surely?'

I assured him they did. He looked suspicious.

'The reason I asked,' he said sternly, 'was because we're trying to keep rabbits and scrubbers out of the club. We're tired of people who pretend to be twenty-four and who can't break a hundred.'

I gave a ghastly twitch and spilled my drink over the floor. In my pocket was a card for the round I had just completed. It totalled 108 and I thought it so good I'd just bought everyone drinks on the strength of it.

So remember the imaginary golf society may prove better than a real one for membership purposes.

People will be needed to support a Coarse Golfer's application. It is not a bad idea if while awaiting election the Coarse Golfer visits the bar with his proposers and is seen drinking lavishly and losing on the fruit machine. Nothing makes a man more popular in a golf club than to pour money into the machine without ever winning. Do not win the jackpot or you may well be blackballed.

Never have a round before the membership application is approved. Inevitably it will be discovered that the player behind, watching impassively as you wreck the loveliest part of the course, will be the club captain whom you last met in the bar when you were boasting about burning up Sunningdale.

Through failure to observe this rule I lost the chance of becoming a member of one of the best clubs in Middlesex.

An old Army friend invited me there. I had last seen him polishing a latrine floor while an N.C.O. stood over him shouting, 'You college-educated nignog', but when I met him by chance in Mayfair he was earning ten thousand a year. After the initial ecstasies of reunion were over we arranged to play golf at his club the following Sunday.

The main sport indulged in at this club on a Sunday seemed to be drink and since I can play that a good deal better than golf I was as good as elected a member by two o'clock. People were scrawling their names all over my application form, and other people's forms by mistake, and I had already rashly announced my handicap as eighteen.

All might yet have been well, if we had not made the mistake of trying to play our arranged round.

The captain himself, with gin coming out of his ears, led us to the first tee while a crowd waving beer glasses watched from the terrace.

Such was my fuddled state that I had difficulty in focusing on the first green. Although the card showed that it was 335 yards away it looked a good deal nearer, but I decided that was the gin because every time I looked the green seemed to be covered in tiny flags.

Realising this was no time for prevaricating, I decided I had to get off before I fell flat on my face. Ignoring such preliminaries as tossing up I therefore put a tee in the ground (which obligingly came up to meet me), put a ball on it, looked at the green, walked up to the ball and hit it.

It was a hole in one.

There was no doubt about it. The ball soared off the face of the club, landed on the green and went down to the accompaniment of a great shout from the throng on the terrace.

Swaying slightly, I looked at the club captain and said what I have always regarded as the wittiest remark of my life: 'I drive better when I'm drunk.'

He looked at me in a peculiar fashion and said nothing.

'A hole in one,' I shouted, 'on my first shot here.'

'Tell me,' said the captain at length, 'do you always need nine chances?'

'What do you mean?' I asked.

My partner put his hand on my arm.

'You idiot,' he hissed, 'you holed out on the putting green.'

In the end they compromised and let me in as a five-day social member. You can't go much lower than that.

Eventually, however, if he perseveres a Coarse Golfer will be elected somehow, somewhere, and awarded a handicap. That is as far as he wishes to go. He is now technically a golfer and if he has any sense the last thing he wants to do is to expose himself in a competition and join that terrible gang on Saturday afternoons, all scoring 40 points in a Stableford.

He merely wants to go on as before, knocking 'em off the tee with an iron and bringing out his woods when there's nobody around.

Unfortunately, some clubs have a habit of reducing a player's handicap by two every year he doesn't enter a competition. While this is a good way of getting down to scratch painlessly, the bubble must eventually burst.

My friend Askew claims to have reached scratch in the following way: when his club reduced his handicap by two he told his office golf society ('in fairness') and they also cut him by two. He then wrote to the golf club ('in fairness') and said the society had just reduced his handicap by two. They immediately cut him by a further two strokes. Askew claims that after endless correspondence he reached scratch without ever setting foot on the course.

A simple way of passing through a competition without trouble is to enter one Monthly Medal with a reliable friend as partner and put in a card that is just respectable. Be careful not to exaggerate. Askew's pride is such that he could not bring himself to put in a card of less than 89 gross and the weather being atrocious he won first prize. Not only that, but he had the cheek to accept it, amid much muttering.

Use the pro frequently. Don't make the fatal mistake of playing a round with him, but just for 'polishing up the swing' so he knows you and nods to you. Be kind to the steward's children, if any, and flattering to his wife, so that if people ask who you are he will say, 'A new member, friend of Mr. Rankin's, nice chap, quiet, unassuming, and quite a useful golfer too, I should imagine.'

Steward's opinions on a player's golf are easily bought.

A Coarse Golfer, being in such a vulnerable position, should avoid controversy at all costs and keep himself above politics and cliques. In this manner he will either obtain a reputation as the biggest two-faced rat in the club, or else be considered a wise, kind Solomon who sees both sides. At the annual meeting he should propose something harmless such as a vote of thanks to the auditors.

A reputation for quiet badinage is useful. This is

Keeping Your Reputation

I AM AFRAID TO ENTER THE **MONTHLY MEDAL**, MIKE, BECAUSE I **DARE NOT PUT** IN MY CARD!

IT WOULD BE SO **BAD** THEY WOULD REALISE I **CHEATED** IN ORDER TO **GET A HANDICAP!**

LATER

A GREAT DRIVE, MIKE — I **CONCEDE** THE HOLE!

DON'T WORRY, ALF! THERE IS A **SIMPLE SOLUTION!**

A SUPERB CHIP, MIKE — I **CONCEDE** THE HOLE!

YOU HAVE GOT THE IDEA **PERFECTLY**, ALF!

BY CONCEDING THE BAD HOLES YOU CAN JUST COUNT **ONE MORE STROKE** THAN YOUR OPPONENT — AND PUT IN A **GOOD CARD!**

not difficult as the standard of humour in the average golf club is rather rudimentary and consists largely of such phrases as 'Aye, aye, watch it, lads, here comes Charlie,' followed by a vacant laugh.

A feature of bar talk is, of course, golfing stories. There are two kinds. First, the alleged joke ('St. Peter and the Devil were playing in the Monthly Medal, you see . . .'). No new golf joke has been invented for forty years so avoid telling them, but listen patiently to other people. Or rather pretend to listen patiently. It doesn't matter if you're staring into space all the time, they won't mind. The teller is not really worried whether anyone is enjoying the joke or not, he just has a compulsion to get it off his chest, and if you won't listen then he'll tell it to the poor steward.

The other kind of story is the alleged true one. The narrator claims to have had some incredible experience, usually involving the landing of the ball in a fantastic place such as a cow's ear.

I once visited three different golf clubs in a week and heard the same story told three times, and each time the teller claimed it happened to *him*. In fact the story had come out of an article I'd written for a newspaper ten days before, and even then it had been a gross exaggeration.

It is bad form, however, to suggest such experiences did not happen to the narrator. As with the golf joke, listen patiently. In fact, such is human nature, people will expect you to tell a similar experience yourself. Unfortunately, any really genuine experience will be dismissed as a thundering lie. I still cannot get people to believe that I really *did* know someone who hit a putt that was certain to go down when a snake slithered across the green and deflected the ball.

Yet Askew has in reserve a walloping great untruth which everyone treats as completely authentic. When he feels called upon to tell his own experiences, he always describes how he played a round with a Prime Minister and beat him three and two, despite the handicap of having six detectives breathing down his neck on every tee.

'Three Secret Service men used to examine the green for booby-traps every time I putted,' says Askew to his spell-bound audience. 'Cables from America were being handed to him in bunkers. In fact he raised the Bank Rate in that sand-trap on the fourteenth. If they would only let him concentrate I think he'd be quite a good golfer.'

This preposterous and totally untrue story has gained Askew a wide reputation as both a golfer and a man of affairs. There must be a lesson there somewhere.

One of the most important tasks for a Coarse Golfer is to make friends with the club secretary. Go on, revolt yourself. The task though difficult, will be rewarding.

Why it should be so difficult to make friends with a golf club secretary I don't know. I remember once playing a round in a society match at a pretty ordinary sort of course and going into the bar with the express purpose of ingratiating myself with the secretary.

I made sure I was properly dressed and sidled up to him in a suitable Uriah Heep manner.

'I really must congratulate you on the condition of your greens,' I said, washing my hands with invisible soap.

He turned round, took one look at me and bellowed:

'Leave the premises immediately, sir!'

It was rather embarrassing because everyone turned round and I humbly asked why.

'You are disgusting those ladies over there!' he boomed.

As I hadn't even spoken to the women I didn't know what to do. I glanced surreptitiously down and noticed that my trousers were still there and then I turned round and asked him if there was anything on my back.

This seemed to outrage him.

'Kindly cease this insulting behaviour and leave,' he repeated. 'And do not come back until you have learned manners in front of ladies.'

I went back to the locker room to collect my kit. On looking in a mirror I discovered what had upset him. I was wearing my hat.

I tore it off and went back to the bar. The secretary was engaged in conversation with our society captain.

'I gather you've got this writer-chappie Michael Green playing for you,' he was saying. 'When he comes in I'd like you to introduce me to him as I think he could get us some good publicity.'

I hope he's satisfied.

If these simple rules are followed a Coarse Golfer will find that within a few years he will have a totally undeserved reputation. Members will say of him : 'He's a dark horse, but by gosh you want to watch out if you play him . . . no, I've never actually played him myself, but the steward was telling me about a game he played last year . . .'

And that is as much as any man can hope for.

II

A Child's Guide to Golf

'When the voices of children are heard on the green
And laughing is heard on the hill. . . .'

BLAKE

*Askew's seven-year-old daughter was recently asked
to write an essay in school on the subject of sport. This
was the result.*

I am going to write about golf. My Daddy plays golf
with Uncle Mike. Uncle Mike is very old, as old as
Daddy. Uncle Mike has to play golf with my Daddy
because he has no children of his own to keep him
amused. I do not like Uncle Mike. He is not as nice
as my other uncle who comes to sleep when Daddy is
away on business.

Uncle Mike used to give me presents sometimes, but
he has stopped since I was sick in the back of his car.
When Daddy and Uncle Mike go to play golf they
come back smelling all funny. Daddy says it is Flowers.

One day Daddy took me to watch him play golf
with Uncle Mike. Mummy made him do it as she had
to have her hair done. Uncle Mike was not pleased and
asked Daddy why he couldn't have left the brat at

home, preferably in the kitchen with all the gas taps turned on.

When they got to the golf course they went into a little room in a big house and changed their clothes and then they came out and waited with a lot of other men while some others hit the ball. They were all old men too.

When a man hit a ball he said 'Shave off' and ran to one side to watch it hit the trees and all the others said, 'Ardluck, Charlie', but secretly I think they were pleased.

When Uncle Mike came to hit the ball he spent a long time waving his big club, and then he lifted it ever so high in the air and dug up a piece of earth with it and he was not pleased because he had been naughty and all the men looked at each other and said, 'Oh dear, what a naughty man.'

And I said, 'Are you digging for worms, Uncle Mike?' and they all laughed and one of them patted my head and said I was a clever girl, but I do not think Uncle Mike was pleased.

After Daddy had had his go he went into a little wood and Uncle Mike went into another little wood to look for their balls. Daddy found his ball under a bush. I got it out for him and he built a little mound of earth and put it on it and then he hit it out of the wood and went to help Uncle Mike who was looking into a drain.

I said to Uncle Mike, 'Daddy just found his ball under a bush and I got it out for him', and Daddy tried to put his hand over my mouth but Uncle Mike said I was a good girl and gave me a sweetie.

Just then some naughty men came up and told Uncle Mike that if he had lost his ball he should let them have their little go, but Uncle Mike was rude.

Then Uncle Mike found his ball and he hit it into the drain again and we had to wait while a lot of other men had their go.

Daddy did not go into the wood again but he took ever such a little club and he went to play in a sand-pit like we have in the school playground only much bigger. Daddy played a lovely game throwing sand all over everywhere so I went into another sandpit next door and built a beautiful sand castle with a real moat.

When I showed it to Daddy he went very red and said, 'Good God, look what the child's done', and he and Uncle Mike went down on their hands and knees and flattened out my castle. While they were doing it a man came along on a sort of mowing machine and he said they ought to be ashamed of themselves and he would report them to the secretary, and Uncle Mike said that word again.

After that Daddy and Uncle Mike went to play on a little piece of flat ground with a lot of sandpits round it and a big stick in the middle and Daddy let me hold the stick. It was in a nasty little hole full of water. So when Uncle Mike hit his ball I stopped it from rolling into the nasty hole and Uncle Mike threw his club at Daddy and it hit him on the knee. Daddy said, 'You can't blame me for what the child does', and Uncle

Mike said the only consolation was that I was as happy as if I was in my right senses.

Then we saw two lady golfers, and they were very old, as old as Mummy, and Uncle Mike said something to Daddy and they went away and whispered and came back laughing.

Then we came to a huge river and Daddy and Uncle Mike tried to see who could get most balls into it and my Daddy won because he hit the river more times, but he did not look pleased. Uncle Mike said would I like to go and look in the river for the balls, preferably in the deepest part, but I did not go.

Then they went to play on a bit with a stick in the middle again. Daddy took out his teeny-weeny club, the one he uses to practise with in the living-room. He stood on the grass near the long stick, and he looked hard at the ball and hard at the long stick and then stood on one leg and then he started to breathe very heavily and then he asked Uncle Mike to stop blinking as the noise of his eyelids upset him.

Well, while Daddy was standing still and breathing hard I saw a squirrel and I whispered it to Uncle Mike, and he said, 'Go and tell Daddy now.' As Daddy was swinging his teeny-weeny club I ran up and I shouted, 'Daddy, Daddy, Daddy, I've just seen a squirrel', and he jumped and he hit the ball ever so hard, much harder than he hits it even with that big club with the lump on the end, and the ball went away into a sandpit.

Then Daddy went all sort of pale and trembly, like Diana Bradshaw when she was sick in the playground, and he kept twitching and muttering, and then he said, 'May God forgive me, but I want to kill my own daughter.'

Uncle Mike said would I pull his little truck for him as that might keep me quiet, and he let me pull the truck and I found it ever so easy and I ran round and round and round one of the long sticks just like a racetrack. But two nasty men came along and shouted at me and Uncle Mike took his little truck away from me and said if I had any more brains I would be half-witted.

Then we got back to where they started and we went into the big house and Daddy gave me a lemonade and Uncle Mike gave me sixpence and I put it into a big machine with coloured lights all over it, and I pressed a handle and a lot of sixpences came out of the bottom. Uncle Mike made a noise as if he was going to be ill and said it was the irony of life and now he had tasted the very dregs.

I shall not play golf when I grow up as it is a stupid, silly game. I told Mummy so when she was bathing me and she said I was quite right but men played it because they were silly, stupid people and Uncle Mike was the silliest and stupidest of them all.

Angela Askew (Form IV)

(There is a note on the end of the manuscript in the teacher's handwriting stating, 'There is no need to try and spell out the exact words used by your Daddy and his friend.')